THIS BOOK BELONGS TO

HOME IS WHERE
THE HEART IS

HOME IS WHERE THE HEART IS

By the Kooler Design Studios

Meredith® Press
New York, New York

For Meredith® Press

Director: Elizabeth P. Rice
Product Development Manager: Patricia Van Note
Editorial Project Manager: Maryanne Bannon
Production Manager: Bill Rose

For Portfolio Graphics

Owners: Jo Packham and Terrece Beesley Woodruff
Staff: Ana Ayala, Lisa Dayton, Tim Fairholm, Susan
Jorgensen, Margaret Shields Marti, Lynda Morrison,
Reva Smith Petersen, Florence Stacey and Nancy
Whitley

For Kooler Design Studios

Donna Kooler, Kevin Burgess, Linda Gillum, Ruth
Houseworth, Lorna McRoden and Nancy Rossi

Photographers: David Allison, Ryne Hazen and
John McIntosh

The photographs in this book were taken at The
Reston Farm Market, Reston, VA; The Laurel Brigade
Inn, Leesburg, VA; and Trends and Traditions, Ogden,
UT. Their friendly cooperation and trust is deeply
appreciated.

ISBN: 0-696-02342-3
First Printing: 1990
Library of Congress Catalog number: 89-063874

Published by Meredith® Press

Distributed by Meredith Corporation,
Des Moines, Iowa.

10 9 8 7 6 5 4 3 2 1

Printed in the United States of America

Donna Kooler's home-away-from-home is her California design studio where she is surrounded by beautifully framed cross-stitch designs, the smell of homemade cookies, and the talk and laughter of her "second family," the staff members of the studio.

Her greatest joy in life is providing an atmosphere that awakens creativity. Her brightly lit studio is painted white so as not to compete with the many colors and hues of floss strewn across the room. Her 13 co-workers gaze through huge 12-foot windows that frame the majestic view of an early morning Martinez mist, delighting in the blues of the Pacific and the greens of nearby Mount Diablo.

Children roam freely through the studio, and artists and other staff members have their favorite books and mementos close at hand. The homey atmosphere, aromatic kitchen, soft background music, and scads of floss overflowing the shelves, help Donna, along with co-designers Kevin Burgess, Linda Gillum, Ruth Houseworth, Lorna McRoden and Nancy Rossi, create the wonderful feeling of "home" in their needlework designs.

Home is a happy and secure state of mind rather than a place to Donna Kooler and her associates. Whether your home is an apartment with a big sheepdog, a Victorian house filled with overstuffed chairs, or even an art studio overlooking the San Francisco Bay, she hopes that the pieces featured in this book will give your house that special touch of color and heart-felt sentiment that makes your home the place your heart is.

Dear Crafter,

Thank you for selecting *Home Is Where the Heart Is: An American Sampler 1991*. This charming book is the third in our series of cross-stitch annual publications, created for people like you—who love to cross-stitch.

As you turn the pages, you'll be enchanted by the timeless designs and decorating ideas for projects that are certain to become your most treasured keepsakes. For each project you will find a clear color chart to help guide you while stitching each delightful design.

We at Meredith Press strive to bring you the highest quality craft books, full of exciting designs, innovative uses for projects, clear instructions, and full color photographs illustrating each project. We are proud to publish *Home Is Where the Heart Is*, and we hope you'll enjoy using it to create projects for your home.

Sincerely,

Pat Van Note

Pat Van Note
Product Development Manager

*Home awakens
memories of crackling
fires, inviting aromas,
open arms and
familiar faces – a
haven of peace and
tranquility where love
abides forever.*

Stitch Count: 153 x 219

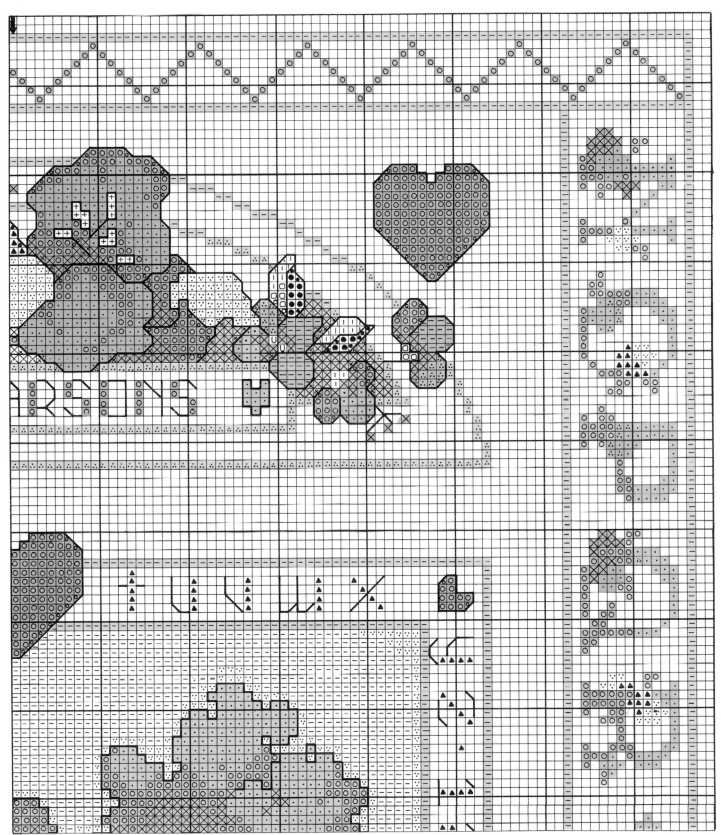

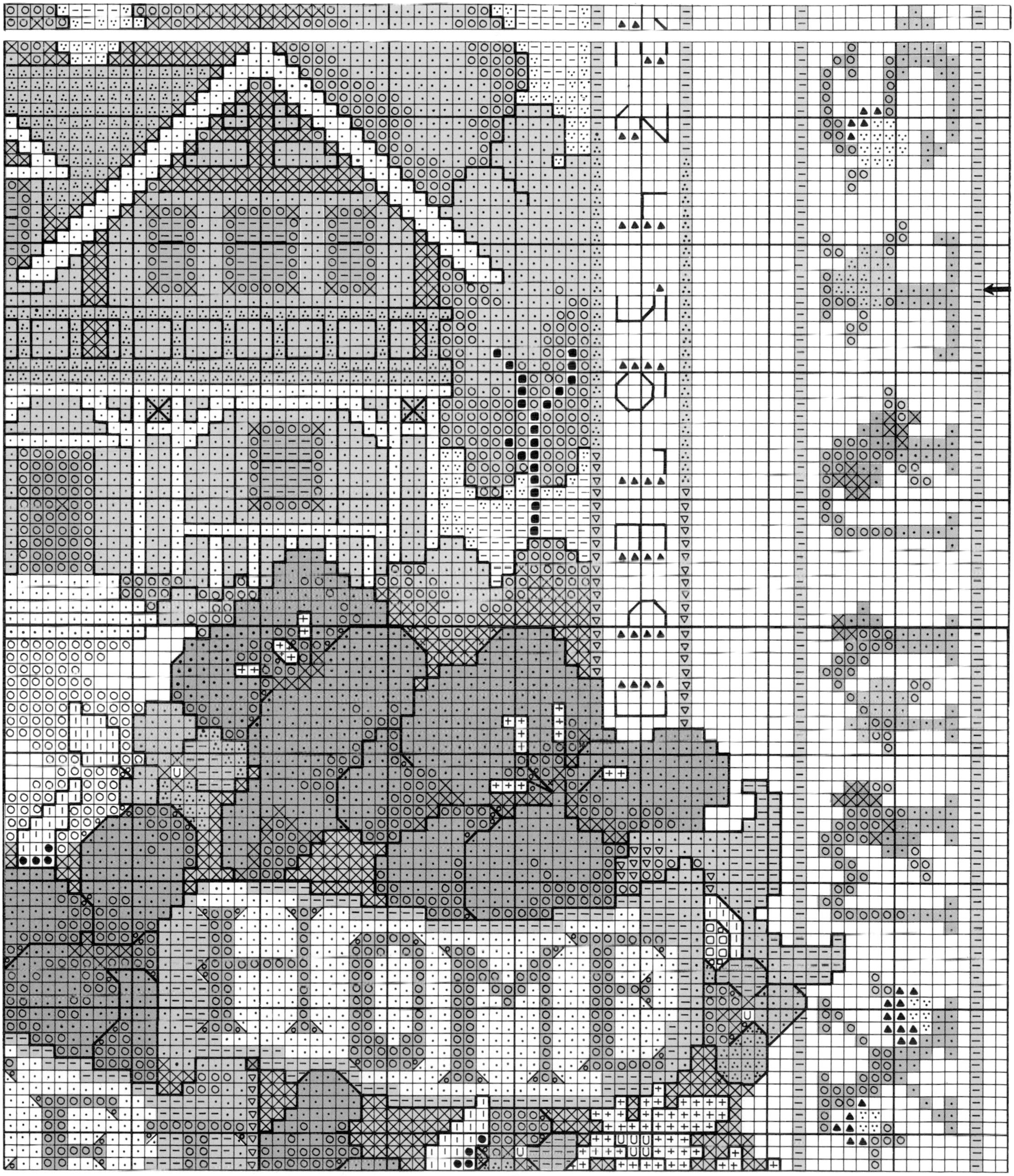

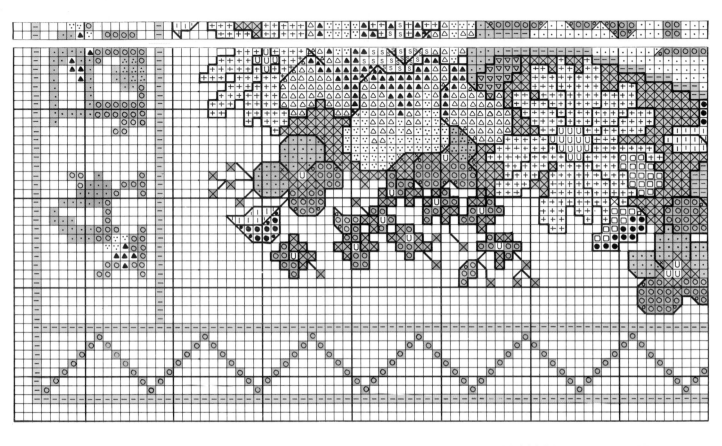

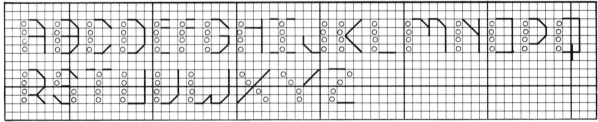

Home Sweet Home

Stitched on Ivory Belfast Linen 32 over two threads, the finished design size is 9½" x 13⅝". The fabric was cut 16" x 20". To personalize the graph, transfer the letters to graph paper. Match center of characters with center of box for family name and begin stitching.

FABRICS
Aida 11
Aida 14
Aida 18
Hardanger 22

DESIGN SIZES
13⅞" x 19⅞"
10⅞" x 15⅝"
8½" x 12"
7" x 10"

Step One: Cross-stitch (two strands)

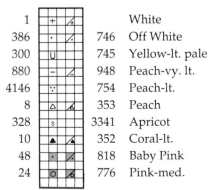

ANCHOR			DMC (used for sample)	
1	+	◿		White
386	·	◿	746	Off White
300	U		745	Yellow-lt. pale
880	−	◿	948	Peach-vy. lt.
4146	∵		754	Peach-lt.
8	△		353	Peach
328	s		3341	Apricot
10	▲	◿	352	Coral-lt.
48	·	◿	818	Baby Pink
24	○		776	Pink-med.

14

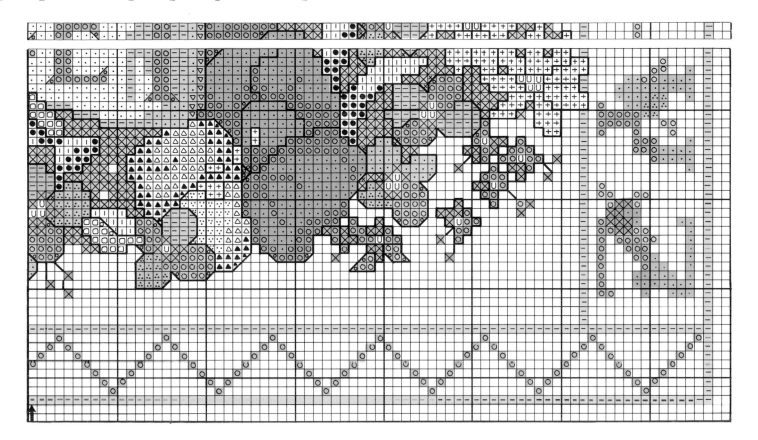

27		899	Rose-med.	
108		211	Lavender-lt.	
104		210	Lavender-med.	
95		554	Violet-lt.	
98		553	Violet-med.	
99		552	Violet-dk.	
128		800	Delft-pale	
120		794	Cornflower Blue-lt.	
121		793	Cornflower Blue-med.	
900		928	Slate Green-lt.	
186		959	Seagreen-med.	
187		958	Seagreen-dk.	
189		991	Aquamarine-dk.	
264		772	Pine Green-lt.	
265		3348	Yellow Green-lt.	
266		3347	Yellow Green-med.	
206		955	Nile Green-lt.	
204		912	Emerald Green-lt.	
229		909	Emerald Green-vy. dk.	
376		842	Beige Brown-vy. lt.	
378		841	Beige Brown-lt.	

885		739	Tan-ultra vy. lt.
942		738	Tan-vy. lt.
362		437	Tan-lt.
363		436	Tan
347		402	Mahogany-vy. lt.
324		922	Copper-lt.

Step Two: Backstitch (one strand)

10		352	Coral-lt. (peach flowers, alphabet, numbers)
27		899	Rose-med. (pink flowers, hearts, name)
98		553	Violet-med. (violet flowers)
121		793	Cornflower Blue-med. (blue flowers, inside windows)
229		909	Emerald Green-vy. dk. (trees, stems, leaves)
362		437	Tan-lt. (white flowers)
363		436	Tan (banners)
324		922	Copper-lt. (house)

Holidays are a time for
making memories – a time
of homecoming when the
family reacquaints itself
with its traditions,
renewing them, building
on them, and passing them
along to the new
generation.

Stitch Count: 159 x 234

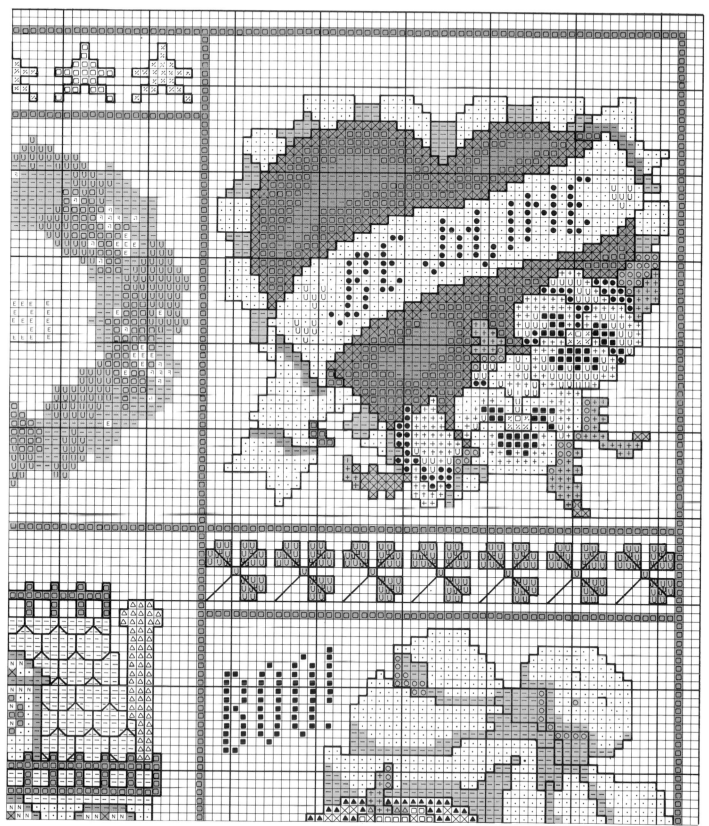

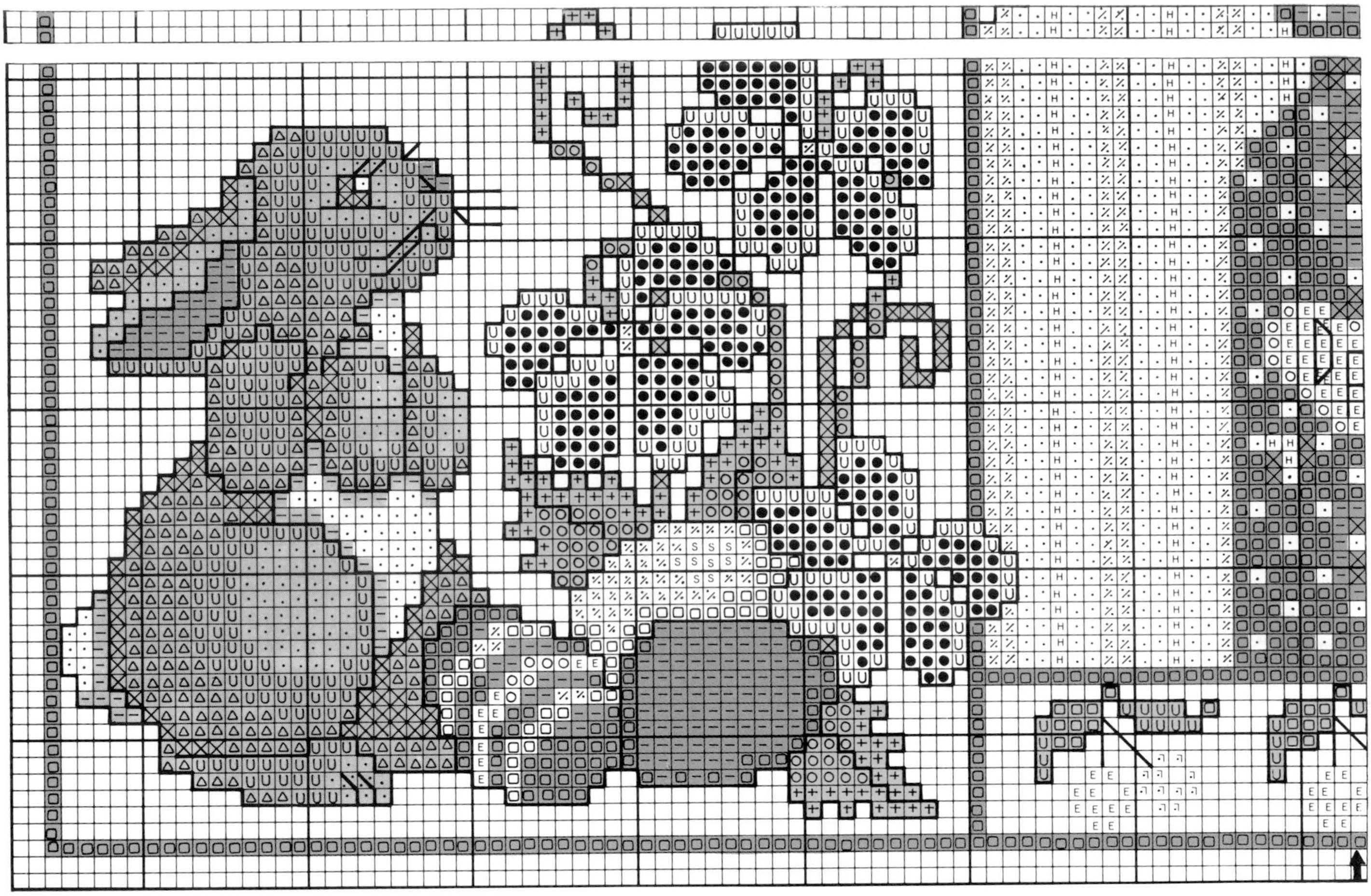

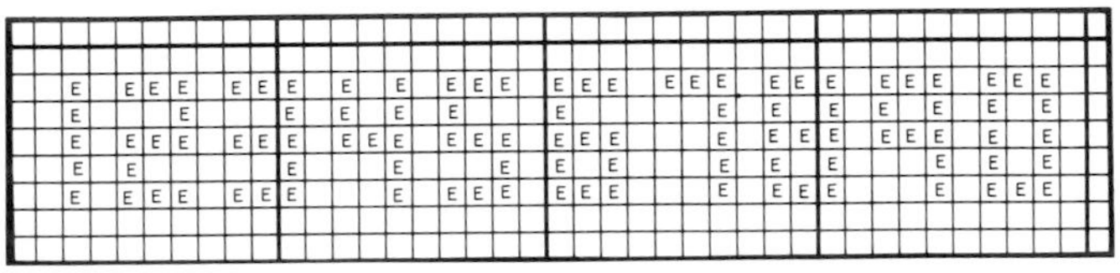

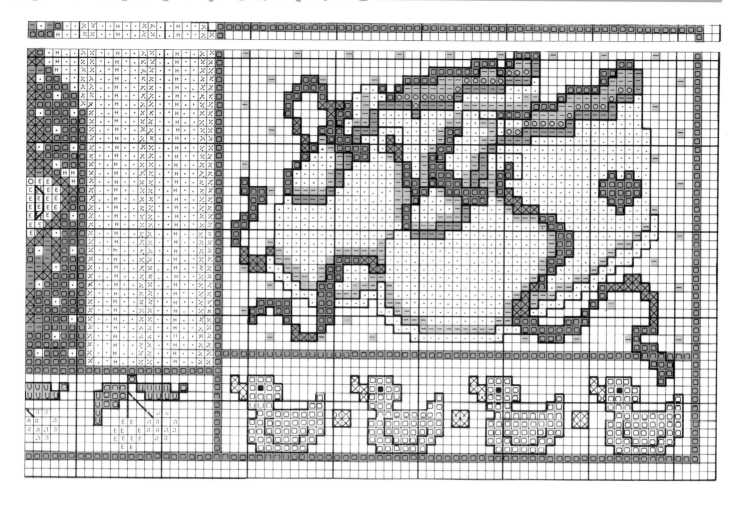

Home for the Holidays

Stitched on yellow Dublin Linen 25 over two threads, the finished design size is 12¾" x 18¾". The fabric was cut 19" x 25". To personalize the graph, transfer the numbers (page 22) for the correct date to graph paper. Match center of characters with center of wreath and begin stitching.

FABRICS	DESIGN SIZES
Aida 11	14½" x 21¼"
Aida 14	11⅜" x 16¾"
Aida 18	8⅞" x 13"
Hardanger 22	7¼" x 10⅝"

Step One: Cross-stitch (two strands)

ANCHOR		DMC	(used for sample)
1	·		White
293	S	727	Topaz-vy. lt.
297	½	743	Yellow-med.
303	▣	742	Tangerine-lt.
316	✕	740	Tangerine
4146	∴ /	754	Peach-lt.
9	○	352	Coral-lt.
10	R	351	Coral
11	✎	3328	Salmon-dk.
13	E	349	Coral-dk.
44	⌐	814	Garnet-dk.
48	▬	818	Baby Pink

23

24	◘	776	Pink-med.
27	✕	899	Rose-med.
117	+	341	Blue Violet-lt.
118	U	340	Blue Violet-med.
119	●	333	Blue Violet-dk.
159	–	827	Blue-vy. lt.
161	◻	826	Blue-med.
149	✕	336	Navy Blue
256	–	704	Chartreuse-bright
239	U	702	Kelly Green
923	◻	699	Christmas Green
264	·	772	Pine Green-lt.
266	+	3347	Yellow Green-med.
257	○	3346	Hunter Green
268	∴	3345	Hunter Green-dk.
246	✕	895	Christmas Green-dk.
886	N	3047	Yellow Beige-lt.
887	·	3046	Yellow Beige-med.
373	U	3045	Yellow Beige-dk.
944	△	869	Hazel Nut Brown-vy. dk.
308	H	782	Topaz-med.
326	▲	720	Orange Spice-dk.
324	–	922	Copper-lt.
339	M	920	Copper-med.
341	△	919	Red Copper
905	✕	3781	Mocha Brown-dk.
382	G	3371	Black Brown
398	–	415	Pearl Gray
400	○	414	Steel Gray-dk.
403	■	310	Black

239		702	Kelly Green (green egg)
923		699	Christmas Green (cherry leaves)
246		895	Christmas Green-dk. (fruit and vegetable stems, pansy stems, violet stems, pumpkin vines and stems, rose stems, clover)
308		782	Topaz-med. (tie bar)
339		920	Copper-med. (pumpkins, stars, ducks, bride and groom, hair, face and hands)
341		919	Red Copper (shingles and chimneys)
905		3781	Mocha Brown-dk. (rabbit, eggs by rabbit)
382		3371	Black Brown (cornucopia)
398		415	Pearl Gray (background of heart)
400		414	Steel Gray-dk. (bride and groom, cake, bells, house, banner on house, shirt and collar, "BE MINE" banner, ghost)
236		3799	Pewter Gray-vy. dk. (ghost's bow, nose and eyes)
403		310	Black (all else)

Step Two: Backstitch (one strand)

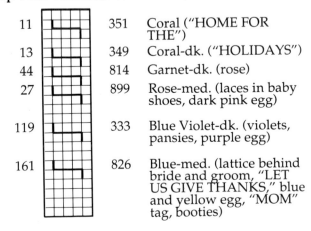

11		351	Coral ("HOME FOR THE")
13		349	Coral-dk. ("HOLIDAYS")
44		814	Garnet-dk. (rose)
27		899	Rose-med. (laces in baby shoes, dark pink egg)
119		333	Blue Violet-dk. (violets, pansies, purple egg)
161		826	Blue-med. (lattice behind bride and groom, "LET US GIVE THANKS," blue and yellow egg, "MOM" tag, booties)

Easter Screen

The design is from "Home for the Holidays" (pages 18-24). The rabbit motif is the box in the lower left corner of the sampler. Stitched on cream Belfast Linen 32 over two threads, the finished design size is 3⅝" x 3". The stitch count is 58 x 48. The fabric was cut 10" x 10". The design was framed in a 6" x 6" frame. The instructions and patterns for the screen and painted design are available from Chapelle Limited; see Suppliers.

A Rose for Mom

The floral design for the doily is from "Home for the Holidays" (pages 18-24). Stitched on white Belfast Linen 32 over two threads, the finished design size is 3¼" x 2¾". The stitch count is 51 x 44. The fabric was cut 9" x 9".

MATERIALS for three heart pillows and doily:
Completed cross-stitch design on white Belfast Linen 32; matching thread
Two 14" x 14" pieces of blue floral print fabric
Two 12" x 12" pieces of blue/white stripe fabric
Two 10" x 10" pieces of blue fabric; matching thread
⅝ yard of 1"-wide flat lace
1½ yards of 1/16"-wide maroon satin ribbon
Maroon beads
Stuffing
Dried flowers
Glue gun and glue

DIRECTIONS:
1. Cut design piece according to DOILY pattern (page 28), centering design. Cut two large HEARTs from floral fabric, two medium HEARTs from blue/white stripe fabric, and two small HEARTs from blue fabric according to patterns (page 28). Set aside.

2. Fold edges of design piece ⅛" double to wrong side and hem by hand. Slipstitch lace to edge of design piece. Adorn lace trim with beads as desired (see photo).

3. With right sides together, stitch large heart pieces together leaving an opening. Turn. Stuff firmly. Slipstitch opening closed. Repeat with remaining heart pieces.

4. Stack heart pillows on top of each other according to size, tacking them together with a few dots of glue. Place design piece over smallest heart and tack (with thread). Wrap ribbon around the two sides and through the cleavage of the heart. Tie ribbon in a bow at center front. Make additional 4"-wide loops with remaining ribbon and tack to first bow. Adorn with dried flowers as desired (see photo).

Halloween Basket Garland

The designs for the garland are from "Home for the Holidays" (pages 18-24).

"BOO!": Stitched on black Aida 18 over one thread, the finished design size is ¾" x ¾" for one motif. The stitch count is 13 x 13. The fabric was cut 8" x 8" for each "BOO!" Stitch two "BOO!" motifs. Replace black floss with a combination of one strand of DMC 720 (Anchor 326) and one strand of 021HL Balger blending filament (see Suppliers).

Pumpkin: Stitched on black Aida 18 over one thread, the finished design size is 2⅞" x 1¾". The stitch count is 51 x 31. The fabric was cut 8" x 8". Stitch one pumpkin motif.

Cat: Stitched on white Aida 18 over one thread, the finished design size is ½" x ⅝". The stitch count is 9 x 11. The fabric was cut 7" x 7" for each cat. Stitch two cat motifs.

MATERIALS:
Five completed cross-stitch designs
One 16" x 7" piece of unstitched white Aida 18; matching thread
One 20" x 8" piece of unstitched black Aida 18; matching thread
6¼ yards of ⅛"-wide orange/white-dot satin ribbon
4¼ yards of ⅛"-wide orange satin ribbon
2½ yards of ¹⁄₁₆"-wide orange satin ribbon
2 yards of 2 ⅛"-wide black satin ribbon
½ yard of ½"-wide black satin ribbon
4½ yards of ⅛"-wide black/white-dot satin ribbon
Stuffing
One basket (model is 9" high, 22" long, 13" wide, 22" handle)
Lightweight wire

DIRECTIONS:
1. Cut one large STAR from design piece, centering pumpkin design. Cut one large STAR from unstitched black Aida for back. Cut two small STAR pieces from design pieces, centering "BOO!" designs. Cut two small Star pieces from unstitched black Aida for backs. Cut one MOON piece from design piece, centering cat design. Flip pattern and repeat. Cut two MOON pieces from unstitched white Aida for backs. (Patterns on page 29.)

2. With right sides together, stitch large star design piece to back, leaving an opening. Trim seam allowances at points. Turn. Stuff firmly. Slipstitch opening closed. Repeat for remaining stars and moons.

3. With all designs facing front, tack one side point and one lower point of one small star to the tips of one moon (see photo). Repeat with remaining small star and moon. Tack side points of large star to center of curved edges on moon.

4. Cut six 12" pieces of orange/white-dot ribbon and six 12" pieces of black/white-dot ribbon. Tie each piece into a small bow leaving 5" tails. Tack one bow

27

of each color in pairs to side points of each star. Curl tails. Cut two 11" pieces of each of the following ribbons: orange/white-dot, ⅛"-wide orange, ¹⁄₁₆"-wide orange, and black/white-dot. Tack one strand of each color to outside points of small stars. Curl tails.

5. Cut two 6" pieces of each of the following ribbons: orange/white-dot, ⅛"-wide orange, ¹⁄₁₆"-wide orange, ½"-wide black, and black/white-dot. Tack one strand of each color to the back of the outside points of both small stars. Tie these ribbons to the basket handle ends to secure.

6. Cut one 44" piece of each of the following ribbons: orange/white-dot, ⅛"-wide orange, ¹⁄₁₆"-wide orange, and black/white-dot. Braid the ribbons around the basket handle as desired, securing at handle ends (see photo).

7. To make bow, cut one 65" piece of 2⅛"-wide black ribbon. Cut two 65" pieces of orange-white dot and ⅛"-wide orange ribbons. Treating all ribbons as one,

fold into five 4"-deep loops, leaving 8" tails (Diagram 1). (It might be helpful to wrap loops around a 4" piece of cardboard). Measure 1" from the end of loops and wrap with wire, leaving 2" wire tails at each end of wire (Diagram 2).

Diagram 1   *Diagram 2*

Curl tails of narrow ribbons. Separate individual loops and shape as desired (see photo). Attach to handle ends with wire tails.

A ROSE FOR MOM
HEART
1 square = 1"

A ROSE FOR MOM
DOILY
Cut 1 from design piece
1 square = 1"

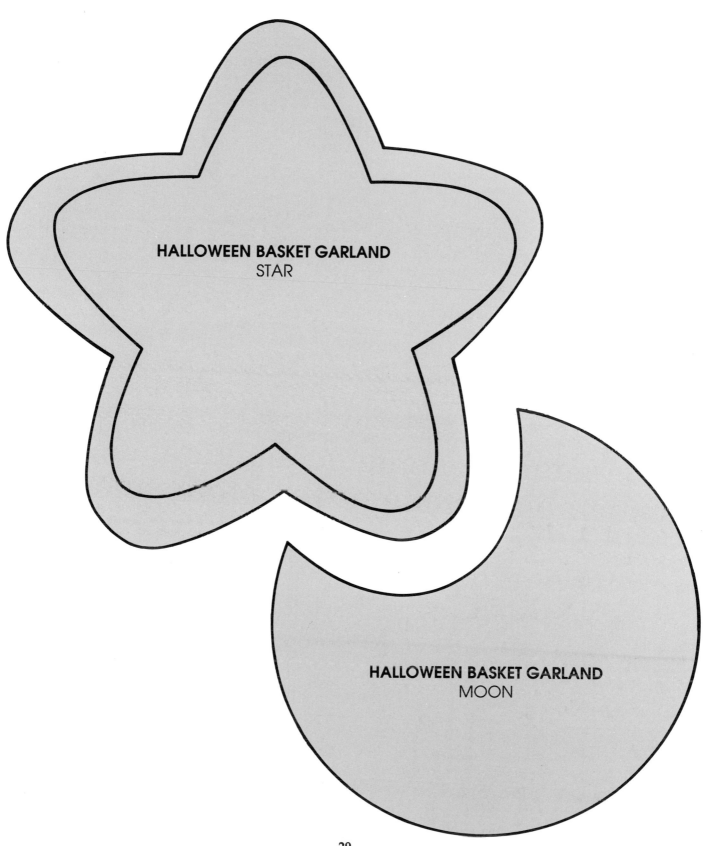

HALLOWEEN BASKET GARLAND
STAR

HALLOWEEN BASKET GARLAND
MOON

Blessed is the home
that welcomes a child,
for the love and
wonder of a child fill
the home with new
life, fresh smiles and
the warm beginnings
of a brand new set of
childhood memories.

Bless This Child

Stitched on white Murano 30 over two threads, the finished design size is 11½" x 8⅛". The fabric was cut 18" x 15". To personalize the graph, transfer the letters for the name and the numbers for the date (page 38) to graph paper. Match center of characters with center of large heart and begin stitching.

FABRICS	DESIGN SIZES
Aida 11	15⅝" x 11⅛"
Aida 14	12¼" x 8¾"
Aida 18	9½" x 6⅞"
Hardanger 22	7⅞"x 5⅝"

Step One: Cross-stitch (two strands)

ANCHOR		DMC	(used for sample)
1			White
300		745	Yellow-lt. pale
301		744	Yellow-pale
4146		754	Peach-lt.
8		353	Peach
881		945	Peach Beige
347		402	Mahogany-vy. lt.
48		818	Baby Pink
49		963	Wild Rose-vy. lt.
50		605	Cranberry-vy. lt.
27		899	Rose-med.
42		335	Rose
108		211	Lavender-lt.
105		209	Lavender-dk.
128		800	Delft-pale
120		794	Cornflower Blue-lt.
121		793	Cornflower Blue-med.
185		964	Seagreen-lt.
186		959	Seagreen-med.
206		955	Nile Green-lt.
203		954	Nile Green
352		300	Mahogany-vy. dk.
398		415	Pearl Gray
401		413	Pewter Gray-dk.

Step Two: Backstitch (one strand)

10		352	Coral -lt. (A, B, C, S, T, U, 9, 0)
27		899	Rose-med. (D, E, F, V, W, 3, 4)
42		335	Rose (large and small hearts, bin blocks, baby bottle tops, peach and yellow flowers, pink and peach flower pots, pink edge of rabbit's ear, horse's mane and tail, bow and heart by horse, name and date, peach section of moon's cap, pink and peach blanket squares, flowers, chimney, windows and door of seagreen house, outline of "Y" block)
105		209	Lavender-dk. (G, H, I, X, Y, Z, 7, 8, bear's ball, rabbit's collar, purple flower, purple squares on blanket, door of peach house, outline of purple house)
120		794	Cornflower Blue-lt. ("A" in block, "Y" in block, J, K, L, P, Q, R, 5, 6, blue "BABY," "BLESS THIS CHILD WITH LOVE AND LAUGHTER," blue heart on horse, trim on saddle, baby chick's cap, outline of blue "B" block)
121		793	Cornflower Blue-med. (border behind rabbit, "BLESS THIS HOME FOR ALL WHO COME AFTER")
186		959	Seagreen-med. (M, N, O, 1, 2, stripe in bear's ball, seagreen flower pot)
189		991	Aquamarine-dk. ("A" block outline, leaves, stems, green squares, on blanket and baby shirt, trees, shutters, door and sides of peach house, shutters and door on purple house)
352		300	Mahogany-vy. dk. (bears, yellow "B" block, chickens, rocker on horse, baby, tree trunks, moon)
401		413	Pewter Grey-dk. (all else)

Step Three: French Knots (one strand)

401   413   Pewter Gray-dk.

Stitch Count: 172 x 123

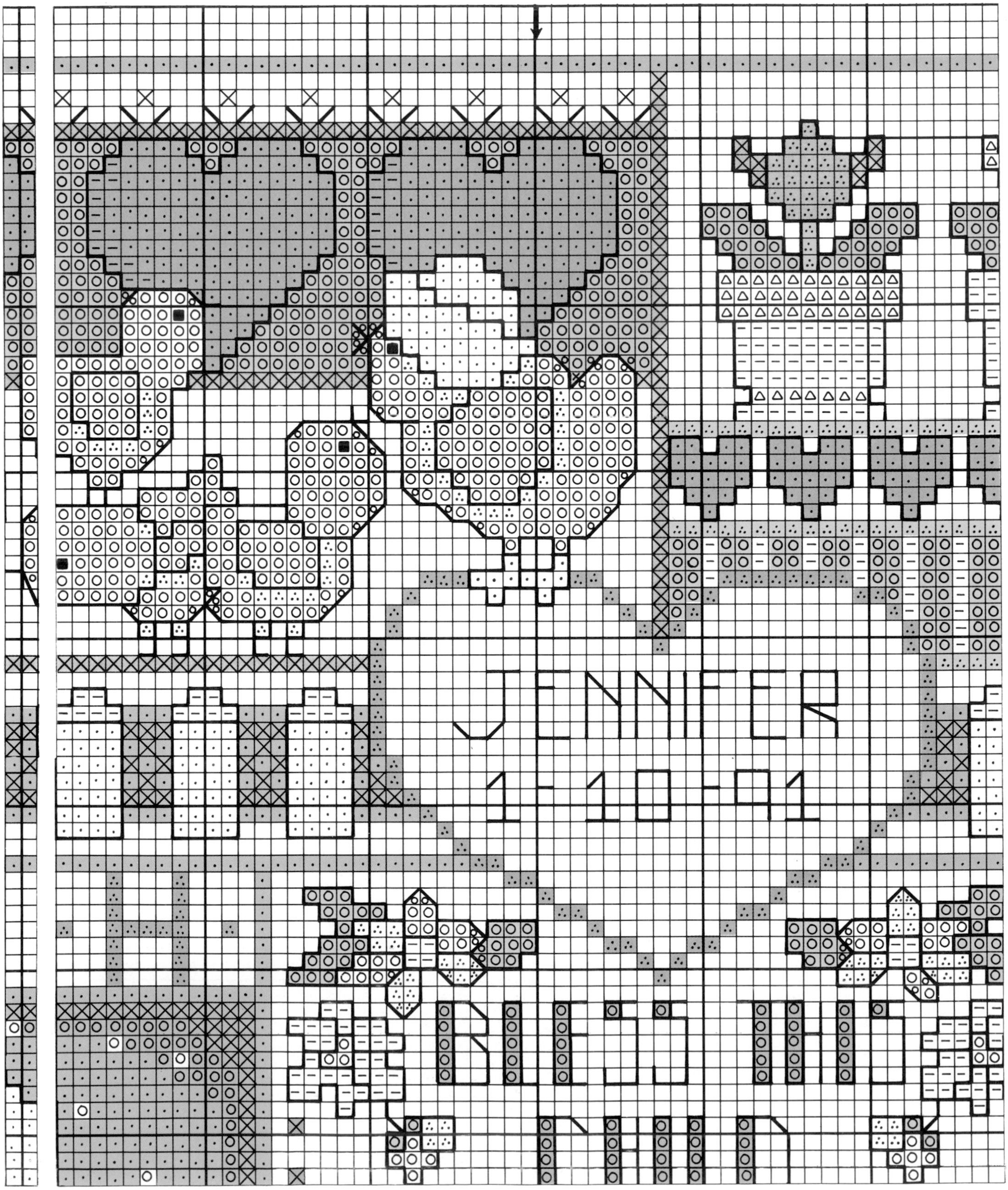
JENNIFER
1-10-91

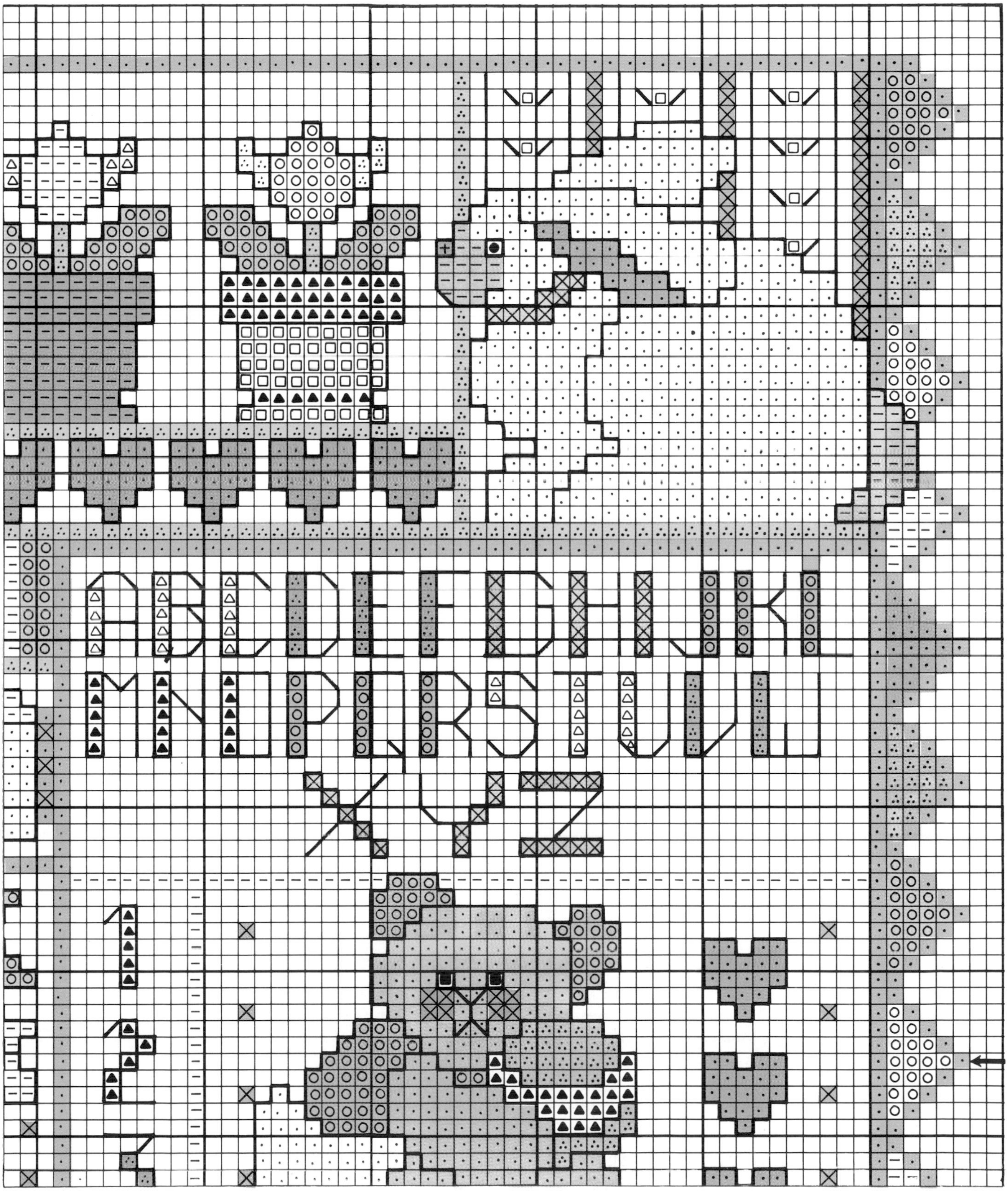

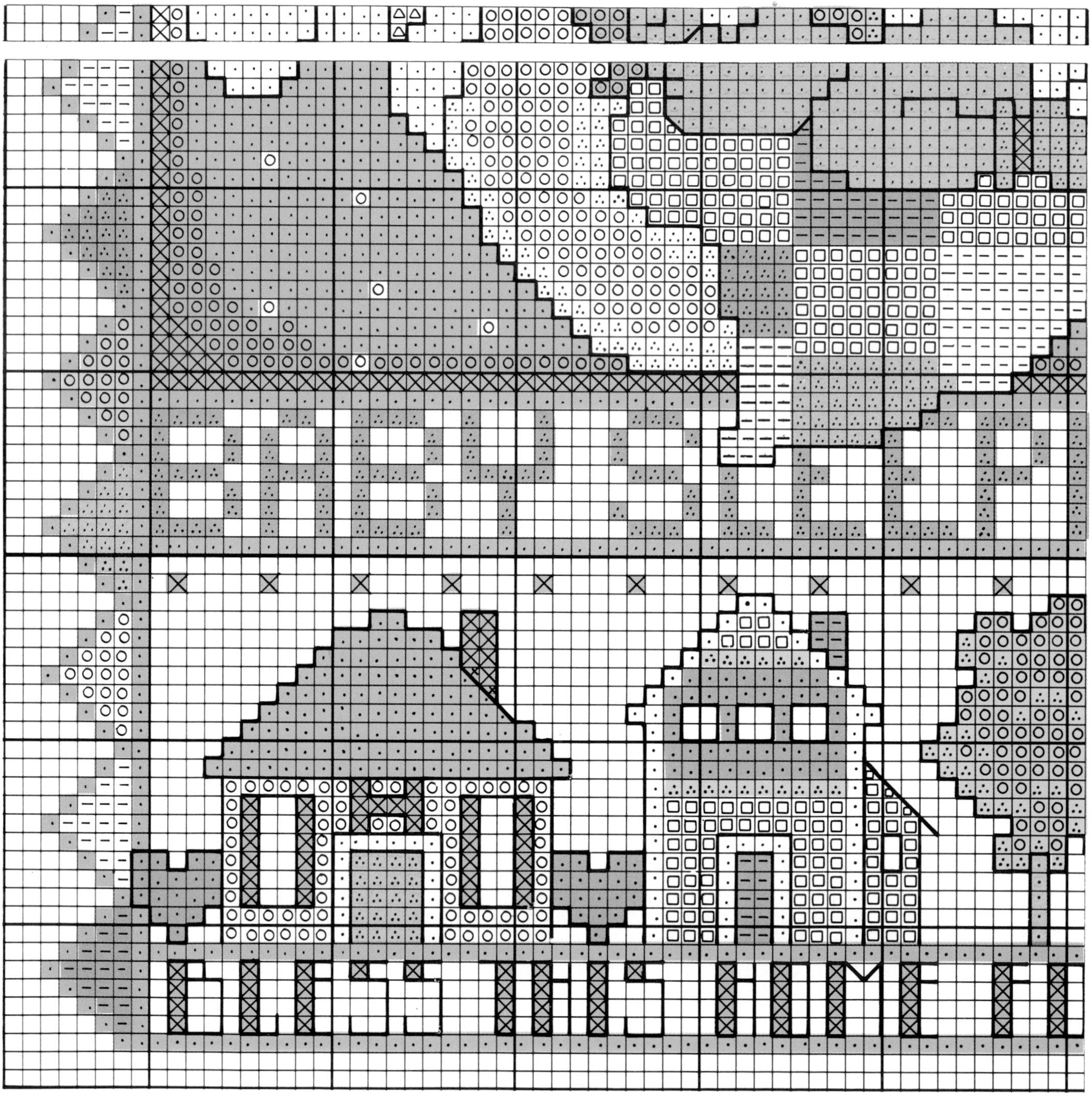

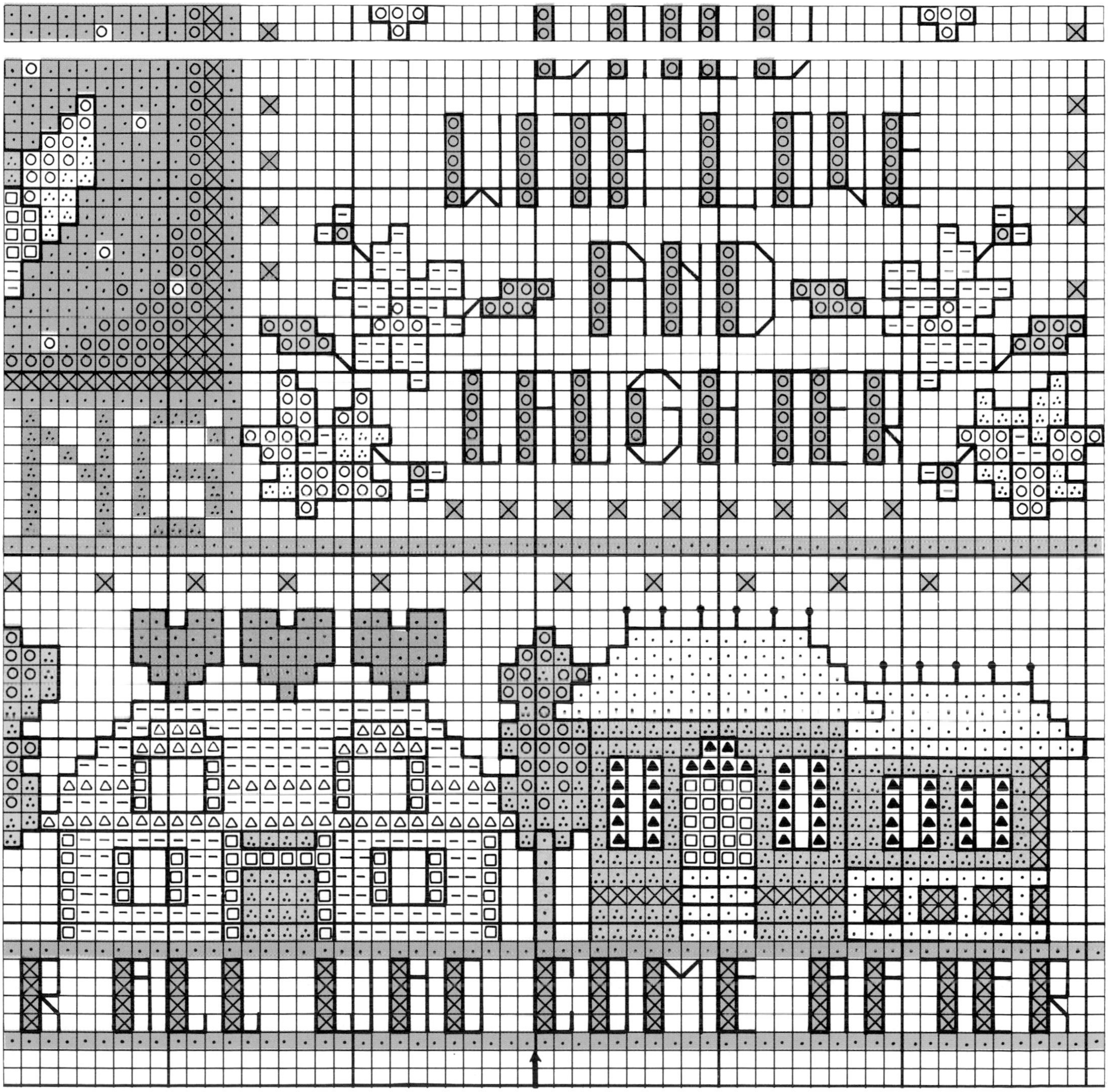
WITH LOVE
AND
LAUGHTER
ALL WHO COME AFTER

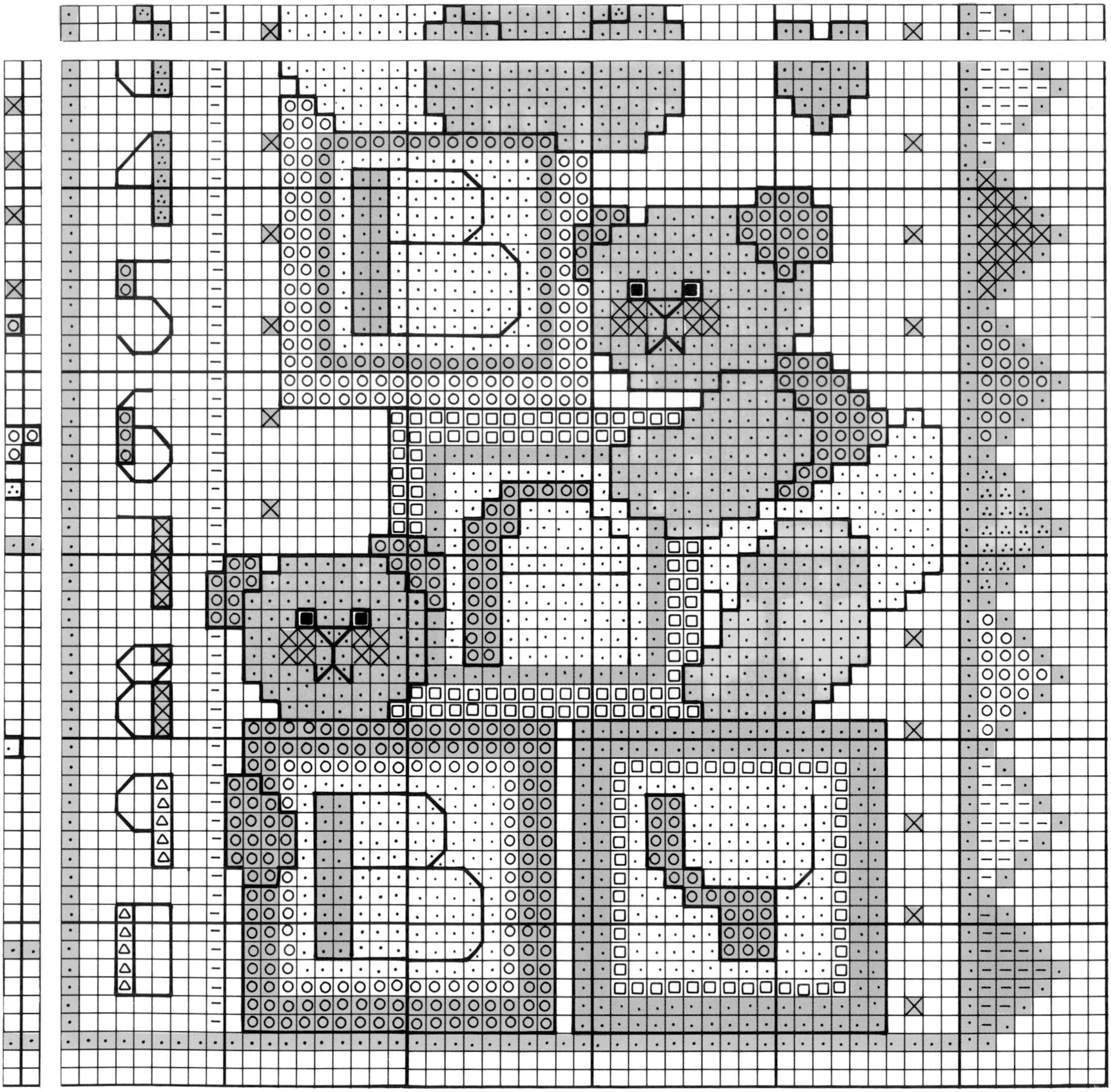

Bear Buddies

The designs for the vests are from "Bless This Child" (pages 32-38). All motifs are stitched on white Murano 30 over two threads. The fabric was cut 5" x 6" for each. The motif for each vest can be placed on either half of the vest front.

Yellow bear vest: The chicken with cap is from the top center section of the sampler. The finished design size is 5/8" x 7/8". The stitch count is 10 x 14.

Green bear vest: The rocking horse is from the top left corner of the sampler. The finished design size is 2⅛" x 2⅞". The stitch count is 31 x 43.

Blue bear vest: The bear on the block is from the lower right corner of the sampler. The finished design size is 1½" x 2½". The stitch count is 23 x 38.

Purple bear vest: The house is from the lower house border of the sampler (last house on the right). The finished design size is 2⅛" x 1¼". The stitch count is 32 x 18.

Pink bear vest: The rabbit motif is from the top right corner of the sampler. The finished design size is 1⅞" x 1⅝". The stitch count is 29 x 24.

MATERIALS for one bear and vest:
Completed cross-stitch design on white Murano 30; matching thread
One 9" x 5" piece of unstitched white Murano 30
¼ yard of polished cotton fabric for bear; matching thread
Five 30 mm doll joints
Two ¼"-wide black shank buttons for eyes
Stuffing

DIRECTIONS for bear:
1. Cut bear BODY, ARMs, LEGs, SOLEs, HEAD SIDEs, HEAD GUSSET and EARs from fabric according to patterns (pages 42-43).

2. To make head, stitch two ear pieces with right sides together, leaving bottom edge open. Turn. Pin a small tuck in both layers of open edge; see pattern. Repeat for second ear. Match A on head gusset to A on one head side piece; stitch with right sides together from A to B; backstitch both ends. Match A on second head side piece to A on other side of head gusset. Stitch with right sides together from A to within 1½" of B; backstitch both ends. Then stitch head side pieces together from A, down neck, across bottom and up to B. Make small slit for ear; see pattern. Insert ear into slit, matching raw edges. Fold head with right sides together and stitch ⅛"-deep dart, securing ear; see pattern. Turn. Insert shank of doll joint in bottom of neck, following manufacturer's instructions. Stuff firmly. Slipstitch opening closed. Sew buttons on seams for eyes (see photo).

3. Stitch two arm pieces with right sides together, leaving an opening. Turn. Insert shank of doll joint; see pattern. Stuff firmly. Slipstitch opening closed. Repeat for second arm.

4. Stitch two leg pieces with right sides together, leaving an opening on one side seam and at the bottom of the leg. Stitch sole to bottom of leg. Turn. Insert shank of doll joint; see pattern. Stuff firmly. Slipstitch opening closed. Repeat for second leg.

5. Stitch two body pieces with right sides together, leaving an opening. Turn. Discarding the doll joint disks, place lock washers only inside body and attach legs, then head and arms. Stuff body firmly. Slipstitch opening closed.

DIRECTIONS for vest:
1. Place pattern for VEST FRONT over design piece, centering the design in the lower half of vest; cut out. Cut second vest front piece and VEST BACK piece from unstitched Murano. Cut vest pieces for lining from fabric to match bear. (Patterns on page 44.)

2. Stitch vest fronts to vest back at shoulders and side seams. Repeat with lining pieces. Place vest and lining with right sides together, matching seams. Stitch outside edges of vest, leaving an opening. Turn. Slipstitch opening closed. Fold seam allowance of armhole inside, clipping as needed, and slipstitch armhole. Repeat for second armhole.

Bear 'n Boot

The design for the boot cuff is from "Bless This Child" (pages 32-38). The house border motif is from the lower left edge of the sampler. Stitched on white Murano 30 over two threads, the finished design size is 7½" x 1⅞". The stitch count is 113 x 28. The fabric was cut 19" x 10". Make one bear from white fabric according to the BEAR BUDDIES instructions (left). The bear is dressed in a pink pinafore.

MATERIALS for pinafore:
¼ yard of pink print fabric; matching thread
½ yard of ¼"-wide green satin ribbon
¾ yard of ⅛"-wide mauve satin ribbon
One ½"-wide pink ribbon rose
One small snap set

DIRECTIONS:
1. From pink fabric, cut RUFFLE pieces according to pattern (page 44). Also cut one 32" x 4" piece for skirt, two 2" squares for bib, two 7" x 1¼" pieces for waistband and four 4½" x 1" pieces for straps.

2. Fold a narrow hem in curved edge of one ruffle piece; stitch. Stitch gathering threads on straight edge of ruffle and gather to equal 4". Repeat. Aligning raw edges, sandwich one ruffle between two strap strips with right sides together, and with ruffle ¼" from both ends of strap. Stitch long edge, catching ruffle in seam. Trim seam allowances. Turn. Repeat for other strap.

3. With right sides of bib front and lining together, stitch top edge. Turn. Sandwich one edge of bib between strap strips, aligning all bottom edges. Fold raw edges of strap ¼" to the inside. Topstitch both long edges. Repeat with other side.

4. Mark centers of bib and both long edges of waistband pieces. Sandwich bib between two waistband pieces with right sides together, matching center marks. Stitch long edge and ends of waistband. Clip corners and turn.

5. Fold skirt in half to equal 16" wide. Stitch along short ends to within 1" of top edge; backstitch. Press seam open. (This seam is the center back seam; the long edge with the opening will be the waist.)

6. Mark center front of the skirt at the waist. Stitch gathering threads in waist of skirt. Fold ¼" hem double to the wrong side along lower edge of the skirt. Hem by hand or machine.

7. Mark center front of the bodice at the waist. Gather skirt to fit waistband. Stitch skirt to waistband with right sides together and through both layers. Zigzag raw edges.

8. Sew a snap set to ends of waistband. Tack shoulder straps to waistband ¼" from each end.

9. With ribbons, make bows and tack to bear near one ear as desired (see photo).

(continued on page 43)

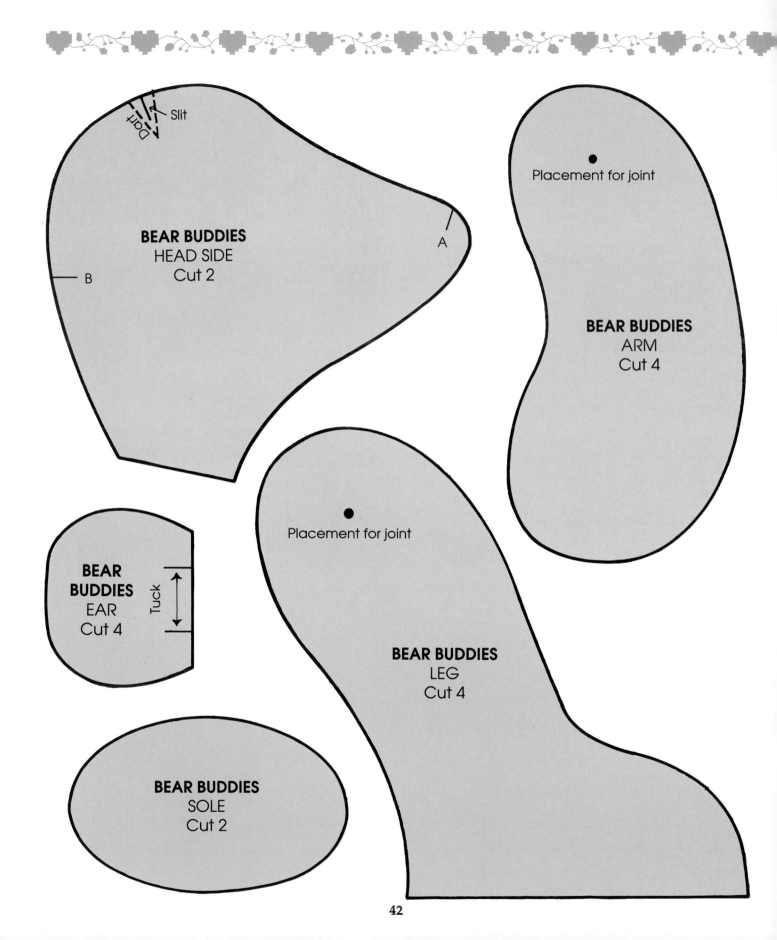

BEAR BUDDIES
HEAD SIDE
Cut 2

Slit

Dart

B

A

BEAR BUDDIES
ARM
Cut 4

Placement for joint

**BEAR
BUDDIES**
EAR
Cut 4

Tuck

BEAR BUDDIES
LEG
Cut 4

Placement for joint

BEAR BUDDIES
SOLE
Cut 2

Bear 'n Boot (continued from page 41)

MATERIALS for one boot:
Completed cross-stitch design on white Murano 30; matching thread
One 6½"-high papier-mâché boot (available at craft stores)
Two 17¾" x 4" pieces of batting
Mint green acrylic paint
Pearl luster spray paint
½ yard of 1"-wide cotton trim
Paint brush
Sandpaper
Glue

DIRECTIONS:
1. Sand seams of papier-mâché boot lightly. Paint boot with acrylic paint; allow to dry. Spray boot with pearl luster. Repeat until desired effect is achieved.

2. Trim design piece to 17¾" x 8½", with design 2" below top 17¾" edge and centered horizontally.

3. Stitch 8½" ends of design piece with right sides together. Fold to measure 17¾" x 4¼" with design right side out. Insert one layer of batting. (Use second layer, if needed, to keep cuff smooth over boot edges.)

4. Fold top raw edges of design piece ¾" to inside top of boot; glue. Glue trim over raw edges on inside of boot.

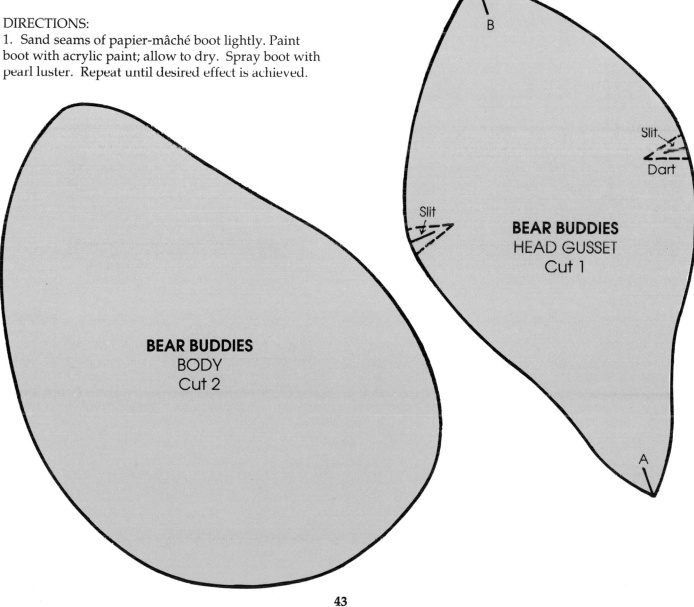

B

Slit

Dart

Slit

BEAR BUDDIES
HEAD GUSSET
Cut 1

BEAR BUDDIES
BODY
Cut 2

A

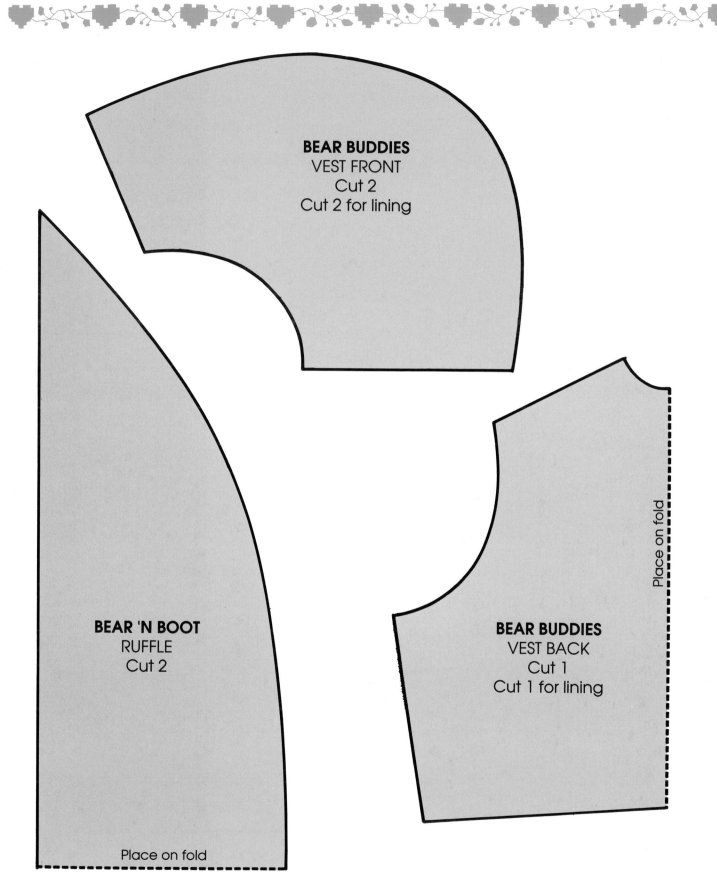

BEAR BUDDIES
VEST FRONT
Cut 2
Cut 2 for lining

BEAR 'N BOOT
RUFFLE
Cut 2

Place on fold

BEAR BUDDIES
VEST BACK
Cut 1
Cut 1 for lining

Place on fold

44

Lullaby Lamp

The designs for the lampshade are from "Bless This Child" (pages 32-38).

"BABY SLEEPING": The motif is from the left middle edge of sampler. Stitched on white Murano 30 over two threads, the finished design size is 4⅜" x 3⅛". The stitch count is 65 x 47. The fabric was cut 8" x 13".

"BABY" blocks: The motif is from the lower right corner of sampler. Stitched on white Murano 30 over two threads, the finished design size is 3⅜" x 6⅞". The stitch count is 50 x 103. The fabric was cut 7" x 18".

MATERIALS for lampshade :
½ yard of Murano 30 (includes two completed cross-stitch designs for lampshade); matching thread
½ yard of white fabric for lining
½ yard of Pattern Pellon™ (available at fabric stores)
Purchased lampshade (the model is 8" high, 8¾" diameter)
Tape

DIRECTIONS:
All seam allowances are ½".

1. Trim "BABY SLEEPING" design panel to 5¼" x 13" with bottom of design 3" from bottom 5¼" edge. Trim "BABY" blocks design panel to 4¼" x 13" with design centered. Cut two 13" square pieces from unstitched Murano.

2. Stitch design panels with right sides together, aligning bottom edges of designs (see photo). Stitch one unstitched piece of Murano to left edge and one to right edge of design piece to make one 35½" x 13" piece; set aside.

3. To make lampshade pattern, mark center of Pellon™. Position center of Pellon™ over center front of shade. Wrap to back and tape edges to shade. Trim Pellon™, matching top and bottom edges of shade. Mark a vertical line at center back. Cut both layers on center back line. Trace shade pattern onto Murano, centering design. Cut out, adding a ½" seam allowance to all edges.

4. To make lining, cut one lampshade piece from white fabric, adding ½" seam allowance. Measure and

mark the inside brace placement on top of lining. Clip top edge of fabric to end of each mark.

5. Stitch center back seams of design piece with right sides together. Repeat for lining. Stitch bottom edges of design piece and lining with right sides together. Turn. Pull design piece over outside of shade, aligning bottom seam with bottom edge of shade. Pull lining piece over inside of lamp. Fold slits for braces under ¼". Slipstitch slits together. Fold top edge of design piece and lining under ½" to the inside. Slipstitch seam closed.

45

To wake to the song of
birds, the sound of running
water and the soft summer
breezes rustling through
the leaves is to be at home
with the Earth.

On the Back Porch

Stitched on ice blue Damask Aida 14 over one thread, the finished design size is 14⅜" x 9¾". The fabric was cut 21" x 16".

FABRICS	DESIGN SIZES
Aida 11	18⅜" x 12½"
Aida 14	14⅜" x 9¾"
Aida 18	11¼" x 7⅝"
Hardanger 22	9⅛" x 6¼"

Step One: Cross-stitch (two strands)

ANCHOR		DMC (used for sample)	
1			White
387		712	Cream
301		744	Yellow-pale
307		977	Golden Brown-lt.
332		946	Burnt Orange-med.
10		352	Coral-lt.
11		351	Coral
13		350	Coral-med.
19		817	Coral Red-vy. dk.
49		963	Wild Rose-vy. lt.
76		961	Wild Rose-vy. dk.
69		3687	Mauve
870		3042	Antique Violet-lt.
871		3041	Antique Violet-med.
101		327	Antique Violet-vy. dk.
158		775	Baby Blue-vy. lt.
121		794	Cornflower Blue-lt.
160		813	Blue-lt.
161		826	Blue-med.
147		312	Navy Blue-lt.
149		311	Navy Blue-med.
265		3348	Yellow Green-lt.
266		3347	Yellow Green-med.
257		3346	Hunter Green
243		988	Forest Green-med.
246		895	Christmas Green-dk.
376		842	Beige Brown-vy. lt.
378		841	Beige Brown-lt.
379		840	Beige Brown-med.
942		738	Tan-vy. lt.
347		402	Mahogany-vy. lt.
338		3776	Mahogany-lt.
352		300	Mahogany-vy. dk.
398		415	Pearl Gray
400		414	Steel Gray-dk.
403		310	Black

Step Two: Backstitch (one strand)

ANCHOR		DMC	
76		961	Wild Rose-vy. dk. (flowers)
257		3346	Hunter Green (light green leaves)
246		895	Christmas Green-dk. (dark green leaves)
378		841	Beige Brown-lt. (trellis)
379		840	Beige Brown-med. (branches)
401		413	Pewter Gray-dk. (cardinal, blue birds, purple bird)
352		300	Mahogany-vy. dk. (all other birds, bird house, border, lettering, flower stems)

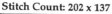

Stitch Count: 202 x 137

49

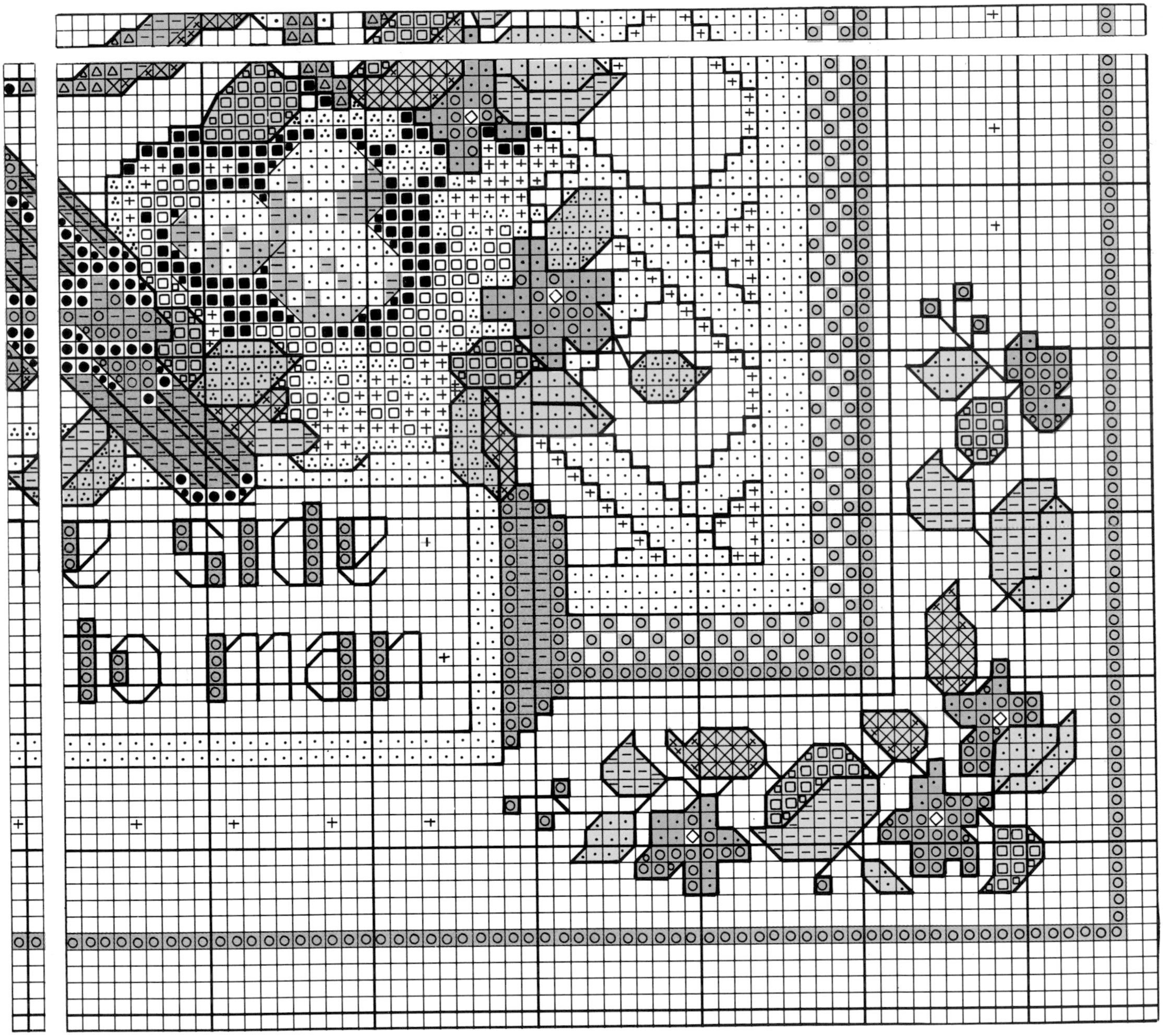
side
to man

Large Floral Sachets

The floral design for the sachet is from "On the Back Porch" (pages 48-54). Choose a small floral motif from the sampler and stitch in the center of a 4" x 4" piece of ice blue damask Aida 18 over one thread.

MATERIALS for one:
Completed cross-stitch on ice blue damask Aida 18; matching thread
½ yard of light blue satin
One 14½" x 8" piece of lace
1 yard of 1/16"-wide satin cord
One 2"-wide covered button hardware set
Large-eyed needle
Glue gun and glue
¼ cup of potpourri

DIRECTIONS:
1. Cut one 2½" circle from design piece, centering design. From satin, cut two 14 ½" x 8" pieces.

2. Baste lace over right side of one satin piece. With right sides together, stitch 8" ends of satin/lace piece together. Stitch 8" ends of second satin piece together for lining.

3. Turn satin/lace piece right side out. Slide satin/lace piece into lining with right sides together. Stitch one 14" edge of satin/lace piece to lining. Turn. Cover button with design piece according to manufacturer's instructions. Stitch gathering threads along 14" raw edge of satin/lace piece. Gather tightly; secure. Attach button to center bottom of sachet over gathering.

4. Pull lining outside sachet. Insert potpourri between satin/lace piece and lining piece. Stitch gathering threads around 14" raw edge of lining. Gather threads tightly; secure. Whipstitch gathered edges together to keep potpourri from spilling out. Push lining inside sachet.

5. For drawstring, sew a running stitch with satin cording 2" from top edge, leaving 6" tails. Gather and tie drawstring in a bow knotting the ends.

Small Floral Sachet

The floral design for the sachet is from "On the Back Porch" (pages 48-54). Choose a small floral motif and stitch in the center of an 8" x 8" piece of ivory damask Aida 18 over one thread.

MATERIALS for one:
Completed cross-stitch on ivory damask Aida 18; matching thread
One 8" x 8" piece of light blue satin
20" of 1/8"-wide cream satin cording
Large-eyed needle
1 tablespoon of potpourri

DIRECTIONS:
1. Cut one 6" circle from design piece, centering design. Cut one 6" circle from light blue satin. With right sides together, stitch design and satin circle together, leaving an opening. Clip curves. Turn. Fill with potpourri. Slipstitch opening closed.

2. For drawstrings, sew a running stitch with satin cording through both layers of fabric ½" from top edge around sachet, leaving 2" tails. Gather and tie drawstring in a bow, knotting ends.

Small Square Sachets

The floral design for the sachet is from "On the Back Porch" (pages 48-54). Choose a small floral motif and stitch in the center of a 5" x 5" piece of ivory or ice blue damask Aida 18 over one thread.

MATERIALS for one :
Completed cross-stitch on damask Aida 18; matching thread
One 2½" square piece of matching unstitched damask Aida 18
Stuffing
1 teaspoon of potpourri

DIRECTIONS:
1. Trim design piece to a 2½" square with design in one corner. With right sides together, stitch design piece and back piece together, leaving an opening. Trim seam allowance at corners. Turn. Stuff firmly with potpourri and stuffing. Slipstitch opening closed.

Optional: Make three sachets and tie them together with a 32" piece of ⅛"-wide satin cording (see photo).

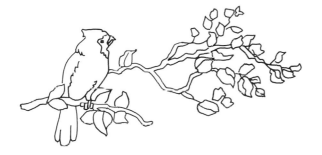

Birdhouse

The birdhouse design is from "On the Back Porch" (page 48-54). Stitched on cream Perforated Paper 14 over one, the finished design size is 2¾" x 3⅛". The stitch count is 39 x 43. The paper was cut 6" x 6". Do not stitch the leaves on the birdhouse. Use the right side of the birdhouse as a guide to replace the leaves with the heart design. (Use three strands of floss for cross-stitching and one for backstitching.)

MATERIALS:
Completed cross-stitch on cream Perforated Paper 14
One 1½" x 2" block of 1¾"-wide wood
One 2" x 3" block of 1¾"-wide wood
1" piece of ⅛"-wide dowel
Drill, ½" drill bit and ⅛" drill bit
Spray adhesive
Wood glue

DIRECTIONS:
1. Cut design piece one hole outside design. Cut two holes in center where indicated on graph (see photo).

2. Cut ROOF from 2" x 3" block of wood according to pattern. Center 1½" x 2" block of wood on bottom of roof piece and glue. Place design piece over house and mark placements for holes with a pencil. Remove design piece and drill holes.

3. Glue design piece to birdhouse front, matching holes. Glue dowel in bottom hole (see photo).

BIRDHOUSE
ROOF
Cut 1

Jewelry Box

The design for the box lid is from "On the Back Porch" (pages 48-54). The motif is the bird and leaves above the nest in the sampler. Stitched on cream Belfast Linen 32 over two threads, the finished design size is 2½" x 2". The stitch count is 41 x 32. The fabric was cut 8" x 8".

MATERIALS:
Completed cross-stitch design on cream Belfast Linen 32; matching thread
¾ yard of cream heavyweight taffeta
¾ yard of 2"-wide cream lace with scalloped edge
2½ yards of ⅛"-wide light blue satin ribbon
2½ yards of ¹⁄₁₆"-wide light blue satin ribbon
1 yard of ¼"-wide light blue picot ribbon
One 4" piece of ⅛"-wide cream satin ribbon
One 22" x 28" piece of poster board
Glue gun and glue

DIRECTIONS:
All seam allowances are 1". To cover poster board with tafetta (or design piece), center fabric over poster board (with batting in between, if called for). Fold fabric seam allowance to other side of poster board; glue, using small amounts of glue.

1. To make heart, cut the following:
   One HEART from design piece, centering pattern over design and adding 1" seam allowance.
   One HEART from batting, ⅛" smaller than pattern (A)
   One HEART from batting, ¼" smaller than pattern (B)
   One HEART from batting, ⅜" smaller than pattern (C)
   One HEART from batting, ⅛" larger than pattern (D)
   One HEART from poster board

Place batting (A) on poster board. Then layer remaining batting in alphabetical order. Cover board with design piece. Stitch gathering threads on the edge of the lace. Gather to equal 12". Glue around heart edges at the back. Set aside.

2. To make box sides, cut the following:
   One 26½" x 5" piece of taffeta
   One 25½" x 1½" piece of poster board

Score lines in poster board (Diagram 1). Fold taffeta in half to equal 26½" x 2½". Insert board into taffeta (Diagram 2). Glue board to taffeta. Fold poster board/taffeta along scored lines to form a 6¼" square. Insert left end into right end overlap. Fold overlap ½" under; glue.

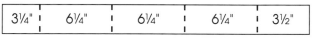

| 3¼" | 6¼" | 6¼" | 6¼" | 3½" |

Diagram 1

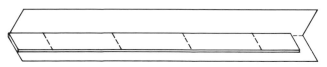

Diagram 2

3. To make box bottom, cut the following:
   One 8¾" square piece of taffeta
   One 6¾" square piece of poster board

Cover poster board with taffeta. Center box sides over unfinished side of box bottom, folding seam allowances toward inside; glue.

4. To make box bottom (inside), cut the following:
   One 8" square piece of taffeta
   One 6" square piece of poster board
   One 6" square piece of batting

Glue batting to poster board. Cover batting/board with taffeta. Glue to box bottom, with unfinished sides together and inside box sides.

5. To make box lid (inside), cut the following:
   One 8" square piece of taffeta
   One 6" square piece of poster board
   One 6" square piece of batting

Glue batting to poster board. Cover with taffeta.

6. To make box lid, cut the following:
   One 9" square piece of taffeta
   One 6¾" square piece of poster board
   One 6⅝" square piece of batting (A)
   One 6½" square piece of batting (B)
   One 6⅜" square piece of batting (C)
   One 6⅞" square piece of batting (D)

Glue batting (A) to poster board. Layer remaining batting in alphabetical order. Cover poster board with taffeta. Center heart over finished side of box lid; glue. Fold cream satin ribbon to make 2" loop. Center and glue ends to unfinished side of box lid edge at bottom of heart (see photo). With unfinished sides together, center box lid (inside) over box lid, catching loop ends in between; glue.

7. Cut one 8" piece of ⅛"-wide blue satin ribbon. Also cut six 15" pieces each of ¹⁄₁₆"-wide and ⅛"-wide blue satin ribbons. Handling 15" ribbons as one unit, make a 3"-deep loop, leaving a 4" tail at each end. Tie 8" piece around center of loop. Glue to bottom point of heart. Separate ribbons, with about half the loops toward the bottom edge of the box. Cut the picot ribbon into three equal lengths. Sew a running stitch close to one edge of each ribbon. Gather tightly to make flowers. Glue over center of loops (see photo).

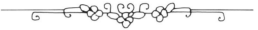

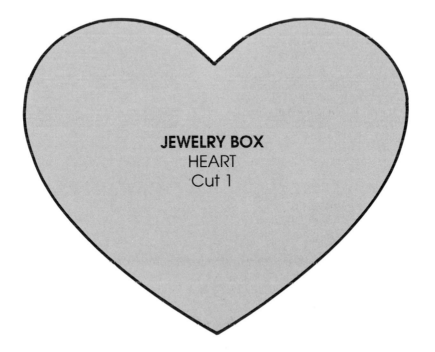

JEWELRY BOX
HEART
Cut 1

The homes that shelter our families are the heart of the neighborhood. All around the town the warm sights and sounds of families living together create an atmosphere of love and harmony.

All Around Town

Stitched on driftwood Belfast Linen 32 over two threads, the finished design size is 14⅝" x 7". The fabric was cut 21" x 13". To personalize the graph, transfer letters for initials and numbers for year (page 67) to graph paper. Match center of characters with center of box and begin stitching.

FABRICS	DESIGN SIZES
Aida 11	21⅜" x 10⅛"
Aida 14	16¾" x 8"
Aida 18	13" x 6¼"
Hardanger 22	10⅝" x 5⅛"

Step One: Cross-stitch (two strands)

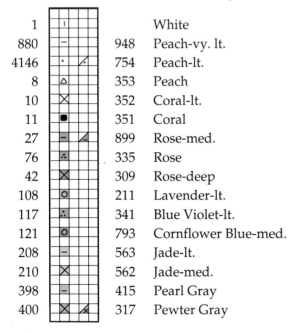

ANCHOR		DMC	(used for sample)
1			White
880		948	Peach-vy. lt.
4146		754	Peach-lt.
8		353	Peach
10		352	Coral-lt.
11		351	Coral
27		899	Rose-med.
76		335	Rose
42		309	Rose-deep
108		211	Lavender-lt.
117		341	Blue Violet-lt.
121		793	Cornflower Blue-med.
208		563	Jade-lt.
210		562	Jade-med.
398		415	Pearl Gray
400		317	Pewter Gray

Step Two: Backstitch (one strand)

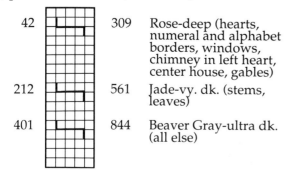

42		309	Rose-deep (hearts, numeral and alphabet borders, windows, chimney in left heart, center house, gables)
212		561	Jade-vy. dk. (stems, leaves)
401		844	Beaver Gray-ultra dk. (all else)

Step Three: French Knots (one strand)

401		844	Beaver Gray-ultra dk.

Step Four: Beadwork (Mill Hill Beads)

	02005	Dusty Rose
	02006	Ice Blue

Santa and His Sack

Design One: The house design is from and follows the same code as "All Around Town" (pages 62-68). The house motif is the last heart/house on the left of the sampler. Stitched on raw linen Belfast Linen 32 over two threads, the finished design size is 3¼" x 2⅝". The stitch count is 35 x 32. The fabric was cut 14" x 10".

Design Two: The "HOME IS WHERE THE HEART IS" graph is on page 68 and follows the code below. Stitched on raw Belfast Linen 32 over two threads, the finished design size is 3¼" x 2½". The fabric was cut 15" x 13". See Step 1 of instructions of the Santa Sack (page 76) before stitching.

Step One: Cross-stitch (two strands)

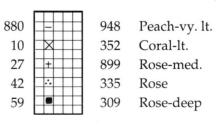

ANCHOR		DMC	(used for sample)
880		948	Peach-vy. lt.
10		352	Coral-lt.
27		899	Rose-med.
42		335	Rose
59		309	Rose-deep

Step Two: Backstitch (one strand)

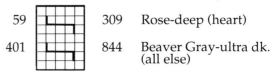

59		309	Rose-deep (heart)
401		844	Beaver Gray-ultra dk. (all else)

Step Three: French Knots (one strand)

401		844	Beaver Gray-ultra dk.

Stitch Count: 235 x 112

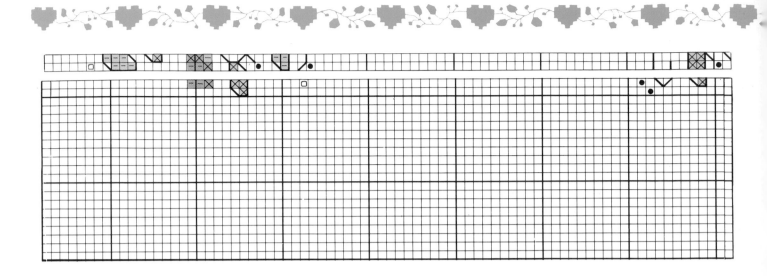

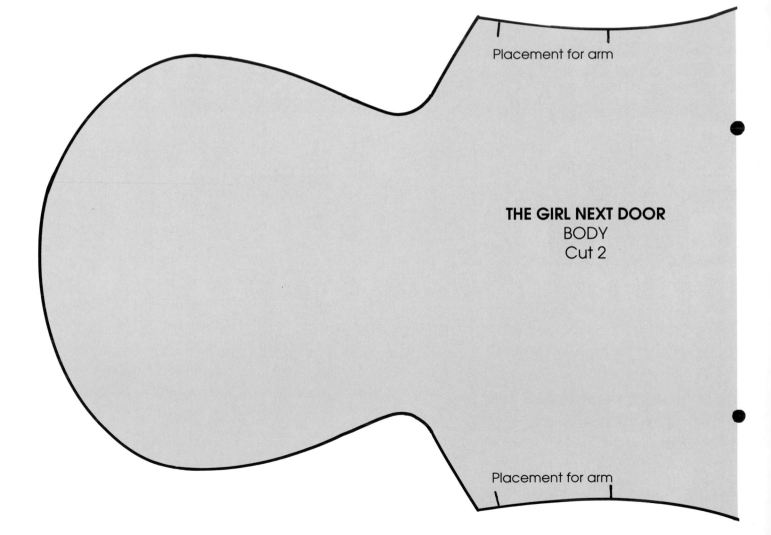

Placement for arm

THE GIRL NEXT DOOR
BODY
Cut 2

Placement for arm

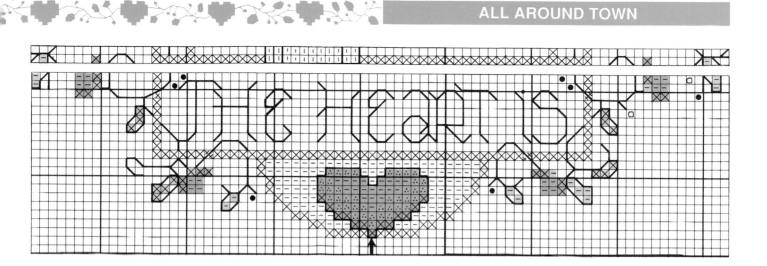

Match patterns
at each

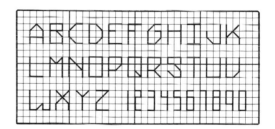

Stitch Count: 51 x 42

The Girl Next Door

The designs for the dress were taken from "All Around Town" (pages 62-68). The four heart/house motifs are used in the same order as they appear on the sampler. Stitched on white Murano 30 over two threads, the finished design size for one heart is 2⅜" x 2⅛". The stitch count is 35 x 32. The fabric was cut 27" x 18". Begin stitching bottom of left heart 3½" from bottom edge of fabric and 10½" from left edge. Stitch hearts ⅜" apart.

MATERIALS for doll body:
½ yard of white fabric; matching thread
One package of craft hair (available at craft stores)
Acrylic paints for face
Stuffing

DIRECTIONS:
1. Cut BODY, LEG and ARM pieces from white fabric according to patterns (pages 66-67 and 72-73).

2. Fold one leg piece in half with right sides together. Stitch long edge and curved edge. Clip curved edge. Turn. Stuff firmly to within 1" of top edge. Repeat for second leg. Stitch two arm pieces with right sides together, leaving top edge open. Clip curves. Turn. Stuff firmly to within 1" of top edge. Fold tuck according to pattern and baste. Repeat for second arm.

3. With right sides together, stitch body pieces leaving openings for arms and legs as indicated on pattern. Clip curves. Turn. Insert arms in side openings. Fold raw edges in ¼" and slipstitch openings closed. Stuff body firmly. Insert legs in bottom opening. Fold raw edges in ¼" and slipstitch entire bottom edge closed.

4. Paint face on doll according to Diagram 1. Dotted lines indicate areas to be shaded. Unbraid and tack hair to doll as desired (see photo).

Diagram 1

MATERIALS for dress and bonnet:
⅝ yard of white Murano 30 (includes completed cross-stitch design); matching thread
⅛ yard of white fabric for bodice lining
1¾ yards of ¹⁄₁₆"-wide white satin ribbon
1 yard of ⅛"-wide white satin ribbon
2¼ yards of ¼"-wide white satin ribbon
3¼ yards of 1¾"-wide white cotton scalloped lace

DIRECTIONS:
1. Trim design piece to 26½" x 17" for skirt with bottom of hearts 3¼" from bottom edge and centered horizontally. Fold skirt to equal 13¼" wide. Cut a "V" shape in the center front of the skirt according to the SKIRT WAISTLINE pattern (next page). Cut the BODICE FRONT, BODICE BACK and SLEEVE pieces from unstitched Murano according to patterns (pages 72-73). Also cut one 5½" x 14" piece for bonnet. Cut BODICE FRONT and BODICE BACK pieces from fabric for lining.

2. Stitch 17" edges of design piece with right sides together to within 2" of waist edge. (This is the center back seam.) Fold skirt in half with seam in center back. Using Diagram 2 as a guide, mark cutting line for bottom edge of skirt.

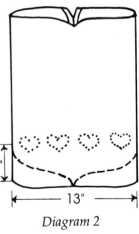

Diagram 2

3. Slipstitch two ⅛"-wide pieces of ribbon on the bodice front and sleeves; see pattern for placement. Slipstitch one ¹⁄₁₆"-wide piece of ribbon on the bodice front and sleeves; see pattern for placement.

4. Stitch bodice front to back at shoulders. Repeat for lining. Cut a 7" piece of lace. Trim lace to ¾" wide. Stitch to neck of Murano bodice. With shoulder seams matching, place Murano and lining bodice with right sides together and lace sandwiched between. Stitch along one center back seam, around neck, and the second center back seam. Clip seam allowance at neck. Turn. Proceed to treat both layers of bodice as one piece of fabric.

5. Stitch a ⅛"-wide hem in the wrist of one sleeve. Stitch gathering threads in sleeve cap. Gather sleeve to fit armhole. Stitch sleeve cap to bodice. Repeat.

6. With right sides together, stitch one side seam and one sleeve. Repeat for remaining side seam and sleeve. Sew elastic thread ¾" above the hem at the wrist, either by hand or with zigzag stitch over thread.

7. Stitch gathering threads along waist edge of skirt. Match center front of skirt to center front of bodice. Gather skirt to fit bodice; stitch. Stitch a ¼" hem in lower edge of skirt.

8. Cut a 2-yard piece of lace. Gather lace to fit hem. Stitch to wrong side of skirt on hemline. Cut a 36" piece of ¼"-wide ribbon. Slipstitch to right side of hemline, mitering ribbon at points.

9. Sew snaps to center back opening at neck and waist of dress.

10. Slipstitch ¼"-wide satin ribbon to waist of dress mitering ribbon at center front.

11. To make bonnet, stitch narrow hems in both 5½" edges and one 14" edge of bonnet piece. (Hemmed 14" edge will be the front of the bonnet.) Fold ¼" double to the wrong side of remaining 14" edge. Stitch to form a casing. Fold a ½"-deep tuck 1" from hemmed 14" edge. Stitch. Press toward casing. Cut one 14" piece of lace.

Sandwich straight edge of lace between tuck and bonnet. Topstitch through all layers along folded edge to form a second casing (Diagram 3).

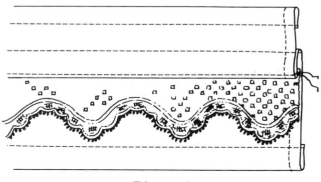

Diagram 3

12. Cut two 14" pieces of lace. Stitch one piece of lace 1" from front edge of bonnet on wrong side. Stitch second piece of lace ¼" from front edge of bonnet on wrong side. Thread 1/16"-wide ribbon through casing on edge of bonnet. Draw up as tightly as possible and tie a knot. Then tie a bow. Trim ends. Thread ¼"-wide ribbon through tuck/casing. Place bonnet on doll head. Draw up ribbon slightly and tie a bow. Tack bow to doll to keep in place.

Place on waistline

THE GIRL NEXT DOOR
SKIRT WAISTLINE

Place on fold

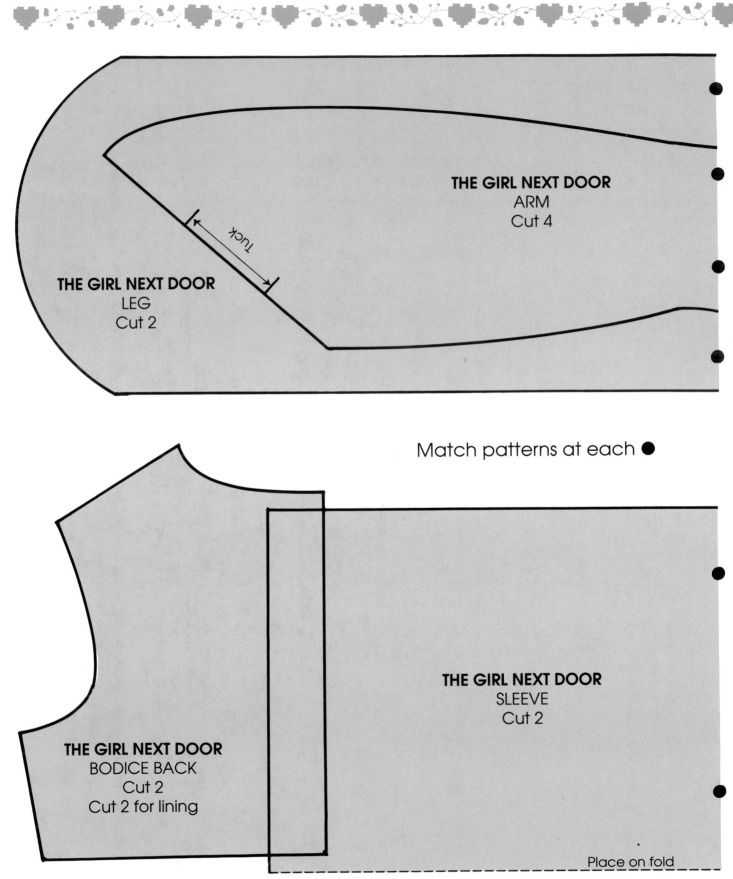

THE GIRL NEXT DOOR
ARM
Cut 4

Tuck

THE GIRL NEXT DOOR
LEG
Cut 2

Match patterns at each ●

THE GIRL NEXT DOOR
SLEEVE
Cut 2

THE GIRL NEXT DOOR
BODICE BACK
Cut 2
Cut 2 for lining

Place on fold

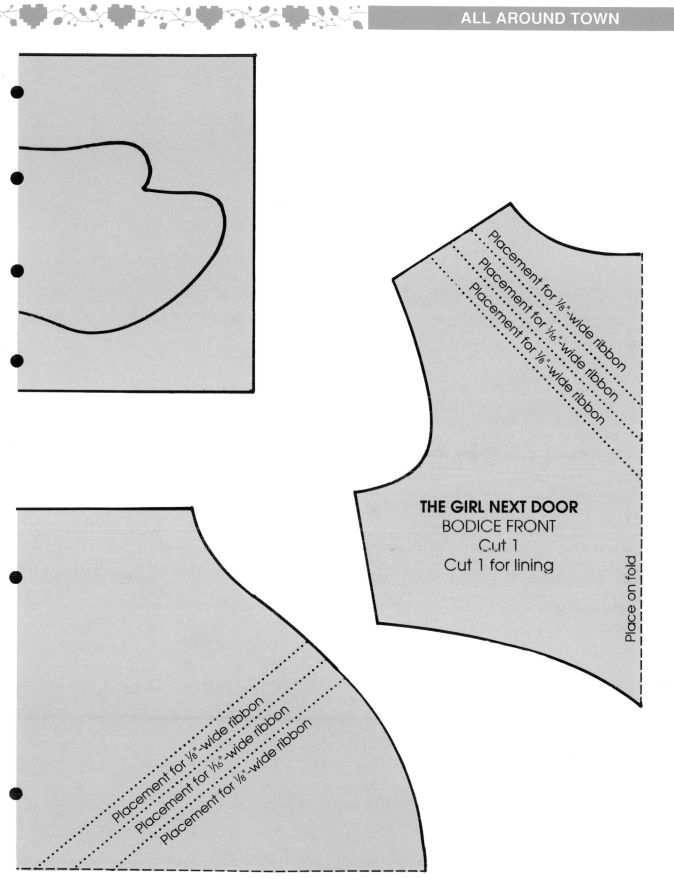

Placement for 1/8"-wide ribbon
Placement for 1/16"-wide ribbon
Placement for 1/8"-wide ribbon

THE GIRL NEXT DOOR
BODICE FRONT
Cut 1
Cut 1 for lining

Place on fold

Placement for 1/8"-wide ribbon
Placement for 1/16"-wide ribbon
Placement for 1/8"-wide ribbon

Spool Horses

The motif for the horses is from "All Around Town" (pages 62-68). The heart is from the small heart border on the sampler. First horse: Stitched on raw Belfast Linen 32 over two threads, the finished design size is ½" x ½". The stitch count is 7 x 7. Second horse: Stitched on Quaker Cloth 28 over two threads, the finished design size is ½" x ½". The stitch count is 7 x 7. The fabric was cut 8" x 4" for both. Stitch one heart motif 2⅝" from each 4" end.

MATERIALS for one:
Completed cross-stitch design; matching thread
One 11" x 7" piece of unstitched fabric (same as design piece)
1 yard of 1/16"-wide pink satin ribbon
7" of unbraided Crepe Hair (see Suppliers)
Two 1⅛"-long wooden spools
Large-eyed needle
Glue gun and glue

DIRECTIONS:
1. Trim design piece to 3¾" x 1½", positioning the bottom of the heart ½" from 1½" end and centered horizontally. Fray ⅜" around all edges for saddle.

2. Cut BODY and INSET pieces from unstitched fabric according to patterns. Cut two 8" pieces from ribbon.

3. With right sides together, zigzag around body leaving the bottom edges open. Stitch inset to one bottom edge of one body piece aligning Xs. Repeat on bottom edge of other body piece, leaving an opening. Turn. Stuff firmly. Slipstitch opening closed. Center saddle on horse back and glue.

4. From unbraided Crepe Hair, cut one 3" piece for tail, one 2" piece for mane and one ½" piece for tuft in front of ear. Glue to horse (see photo).

5. With large-eyed needle, thread one 8" piece of ribbon through the body/inset seam at each triangle; see pattern. Repeat at back of horse. Thread one spool onto each ribbon and tie in a bow on one side so that the spool is secured under horse (see photo). Repeat.

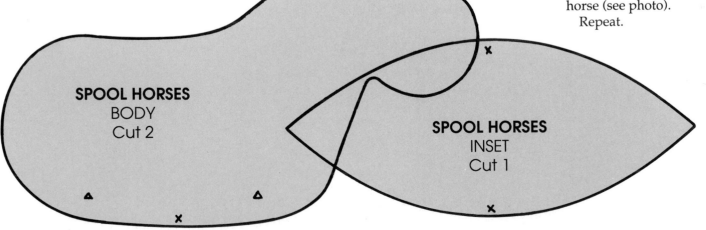

SPOOL HORSES
BODY
Cut 2

SPOOL HORSES
INSET
Cut 1

Santa and His Sack

MATERIALS:
¼ yard of coarse natural-color fabric; matching thread
¼ yard of dark green fabric; matching thread
Scrap of black wool
Scrap of apricot fabric
One ½"-wide jingle bell
6" of unbraided wool Crepe Hair (see Suppliers)
Stuffing
One 1"-wide metal buckle
Small amount of black yarn or floss

DIRECTIONS:
1. Cut pieces for Santa doll as indicated below. (Patterns on pages 76-77.)

    From coarse fabric:
        four ARM pieces
        one 6½"-wide circle for head
    From green fabric:
        two BODY pieces
        one HAT piece
        two 4" x 4¼" pieces for sleeves
    From black fabric:
        four BOOT pieces
    From apricot fabric:
        two 4" x 2" pieces for cuffs
        one 8¾" x 2" piece for hat band
        one 10½" x 2" piece for belt

2. Stitch two body pieces with right sides together, leaving an opening in bottom edge; see pattern. Stitch gathering threads in seam allowance of opening at bottom. Clip curves. Turn. Stuff firmly. Gather and slipstitch opening closed.

3. Stitch two arm pieces with right sides together, leaving short, straight edge open. Turn. Stuff firmly to within 1" of open edge. Baste to hold stuffing. Repeat.

4. Fold cuff piece to measure 4" x 1". Stitch 4" raw edges of cuff to one 4" end of sleeve. Fold sleeve with right sides together to measure 2" x 4¼"; stitch long edge. Turn. Slide sleeve over one arm so that 1" of hand extends beyond cuff. Repeat for second arm and sleeve. Tack arms/sleeves to top of body.

5. Stitch two boot pieces with right sides together, leaving top edge open. Turn. Stuff to within 1" of top. Baste to hold stuffing. Fold ¼" of top edges inside boot and slipstitch opening closed. Repeat. Tack side-by-side to center bottom of body.

6. Zigzag around edge of head piece. Stitch gathering threads on seam allowance. Gather slightly; stuff firmly. Then gather tightly and secure. Tack gathered edge on center top of body.

7. Fold hat band to measure 8¾" x 1". Stitch 8¾" raw edges of band to curved edge of hat. Fold hat piece with right sides together. Stitch long edge. Turn. Sew jingle bell to point.

8. Place hat on head. Mark placement for eyes, mustache, beard and hair. Make two large French knots for eyes. Glue wool Crepe Hair and tack hat as desired.

9. Fold belt piece to measure 10½" x 1". Stitch long edge. Turn. Tack one end around buckle. Place belt on Santa and tack at side seams and center back, fitting belt snugly around Santa as you go. Then tack remaining end of belt around buckle.

MATERIALS for one Santa Sack:
Completed cross-stitch design on raw Belfast Linen 32;
    matching thread (code on page 62, graph on page
    68)
¾ yard of ¼"-wide apricot picot satin ribbon
Stuffing
Assorted small packages and toys

DIRECTIONS:
1. Trim design piece to 13" x 11" with design centered
1½" from bottom 13" edge.

2. With right sides together, fold design piece in half
to equal 6½" x 11". Stitch long edge. With bag still
wrong side out, fold bag flat with seam at center back.
Stitch along bottom edge; press seam open. Stitch
across the corner (Diagram 1). Repeat on opposite
corner. Turn.

3. Fold 3" of top edge to inside of bag. Stuff loosely to
within 1½" of top edge. Tie ribbon loosely around bag.
Place packages and toys in top (see photo).

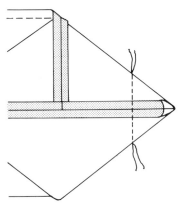

Diagram 1

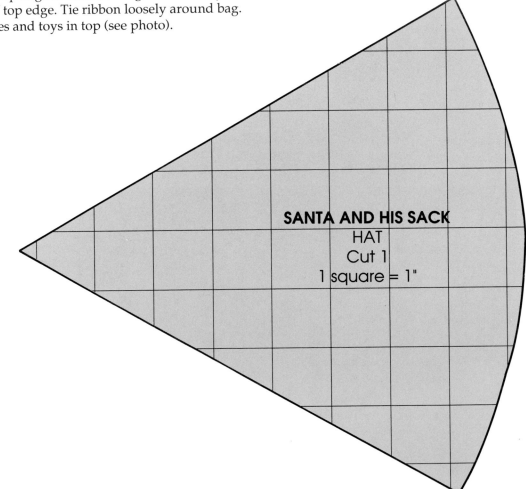

SANTA AND HIS SACK
HAT
Cut 1
1 square = 1"

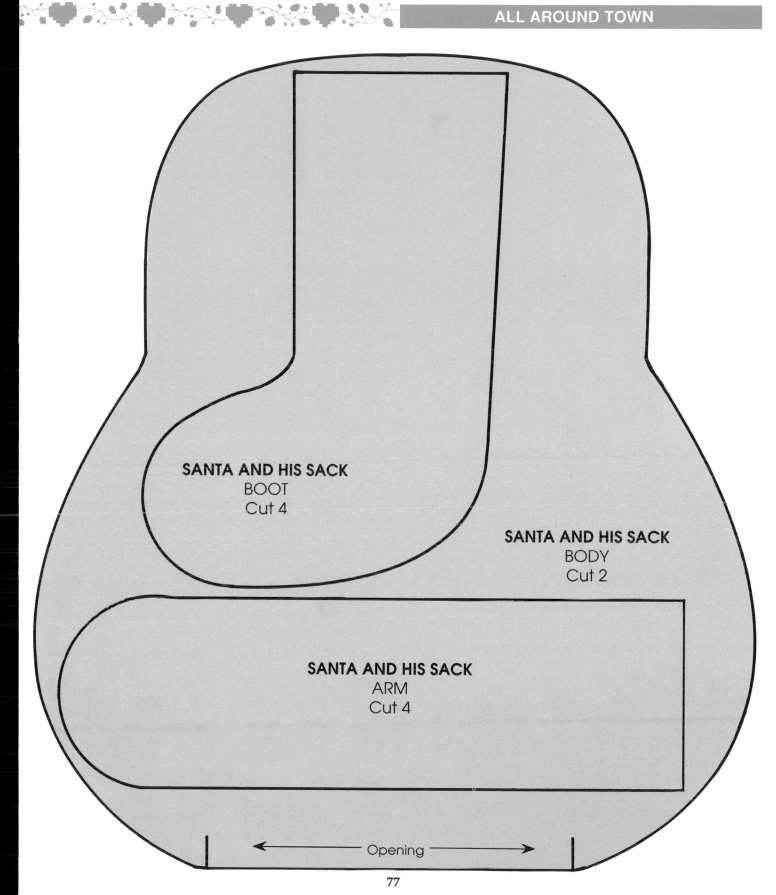

SANTA AND HIS SACK
BOOT
Cut 4

SANTA AND HIS SACK
BODY
Cut 2

SANTA AND HIS SACK
ARM
Cut 4

← Opening →

*Cats purring in the
afternoon sun and bright
summer flowers growing
in the windowsill weave a
delicate tapestry depicting
the pleasures of home.*

Stitch Count: 123 x 192

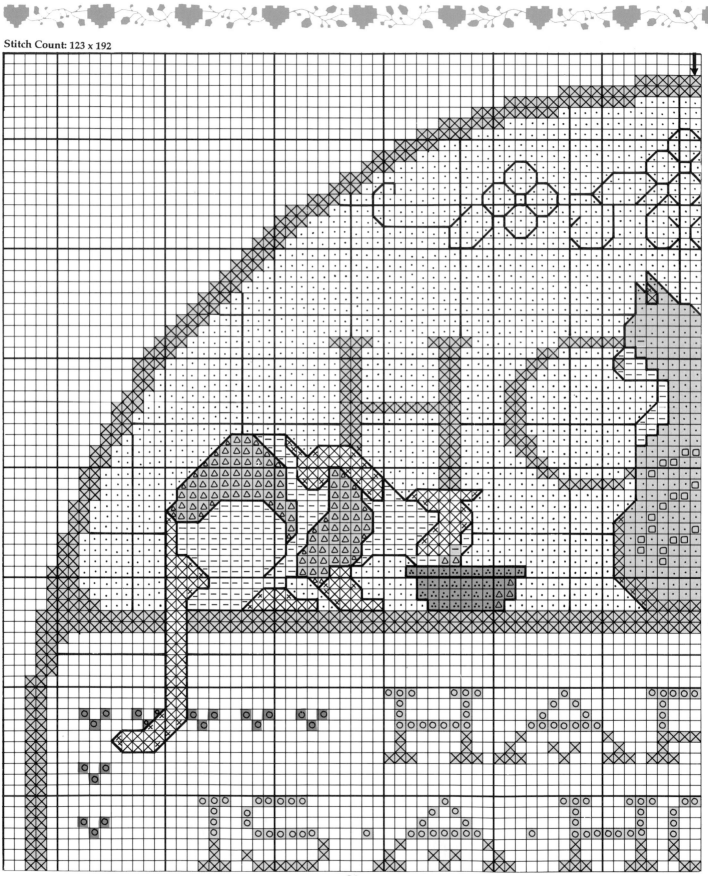

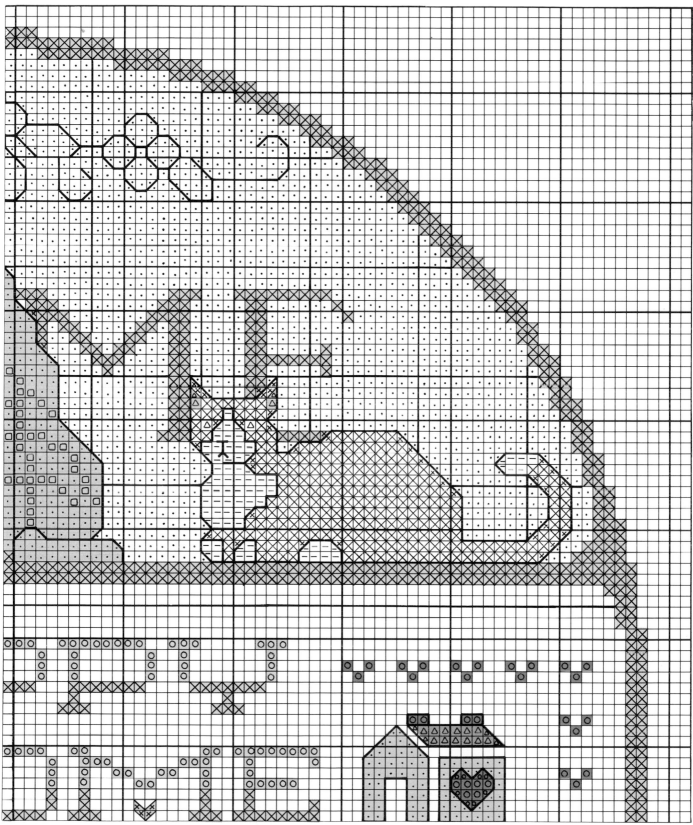

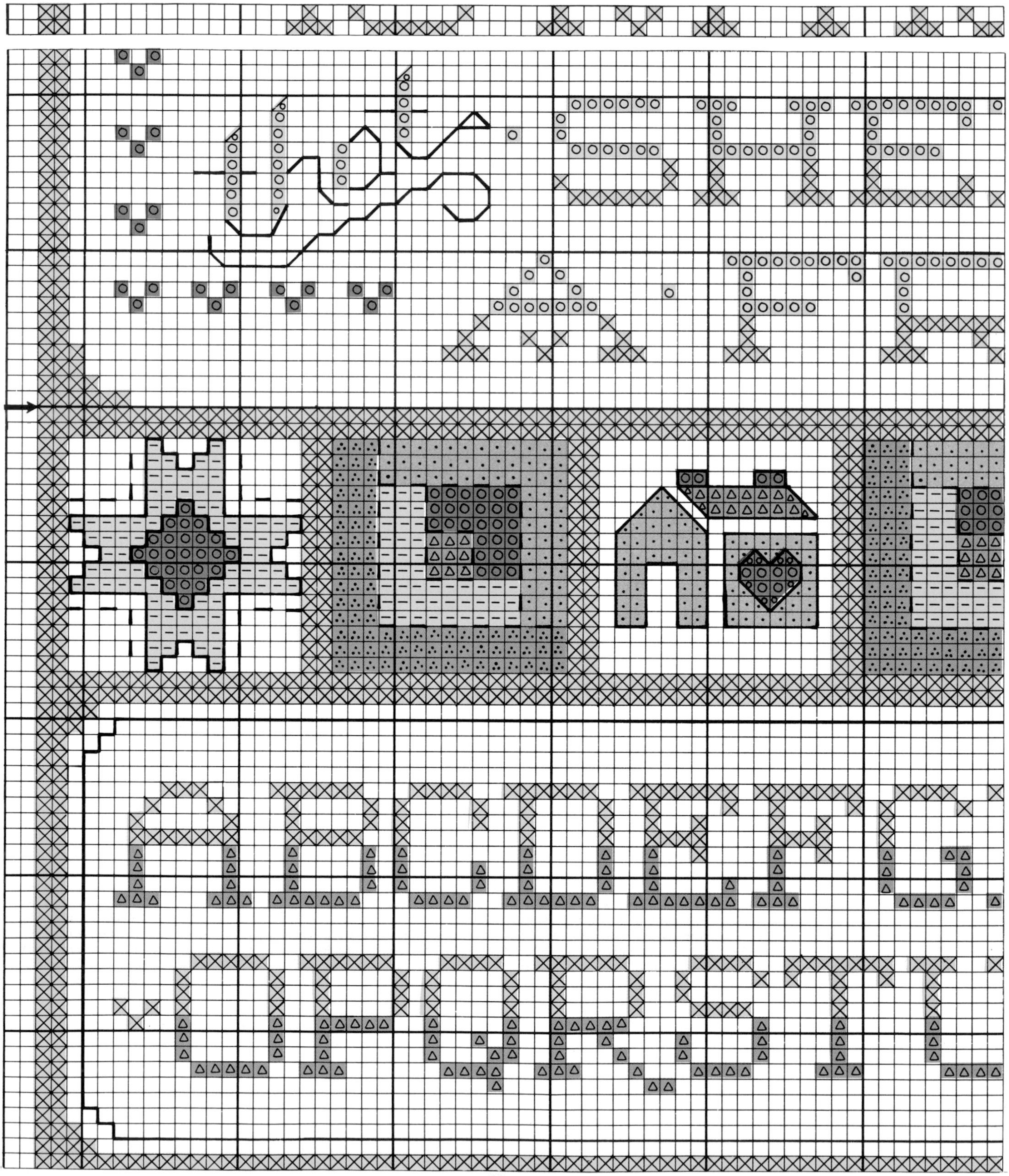

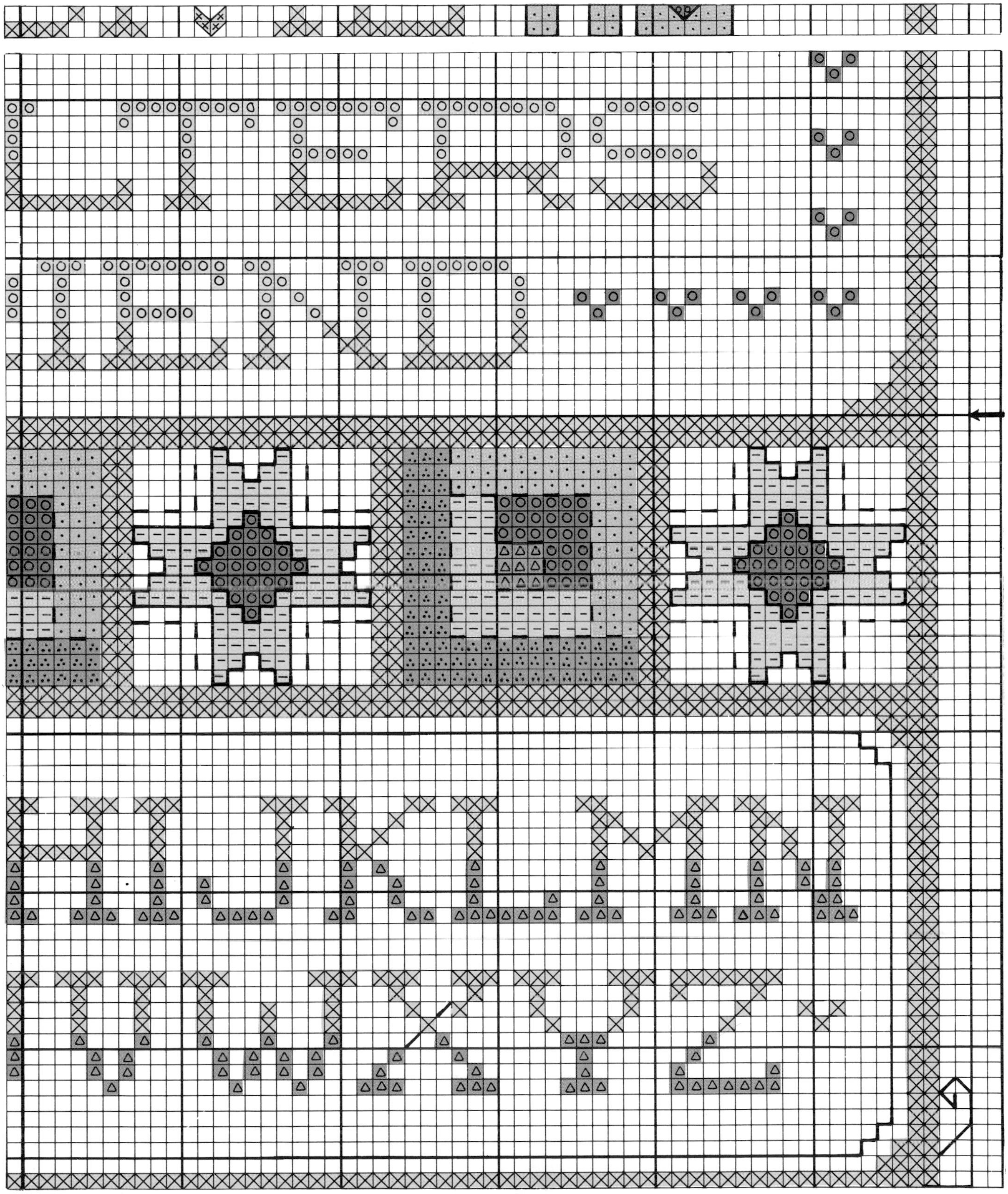

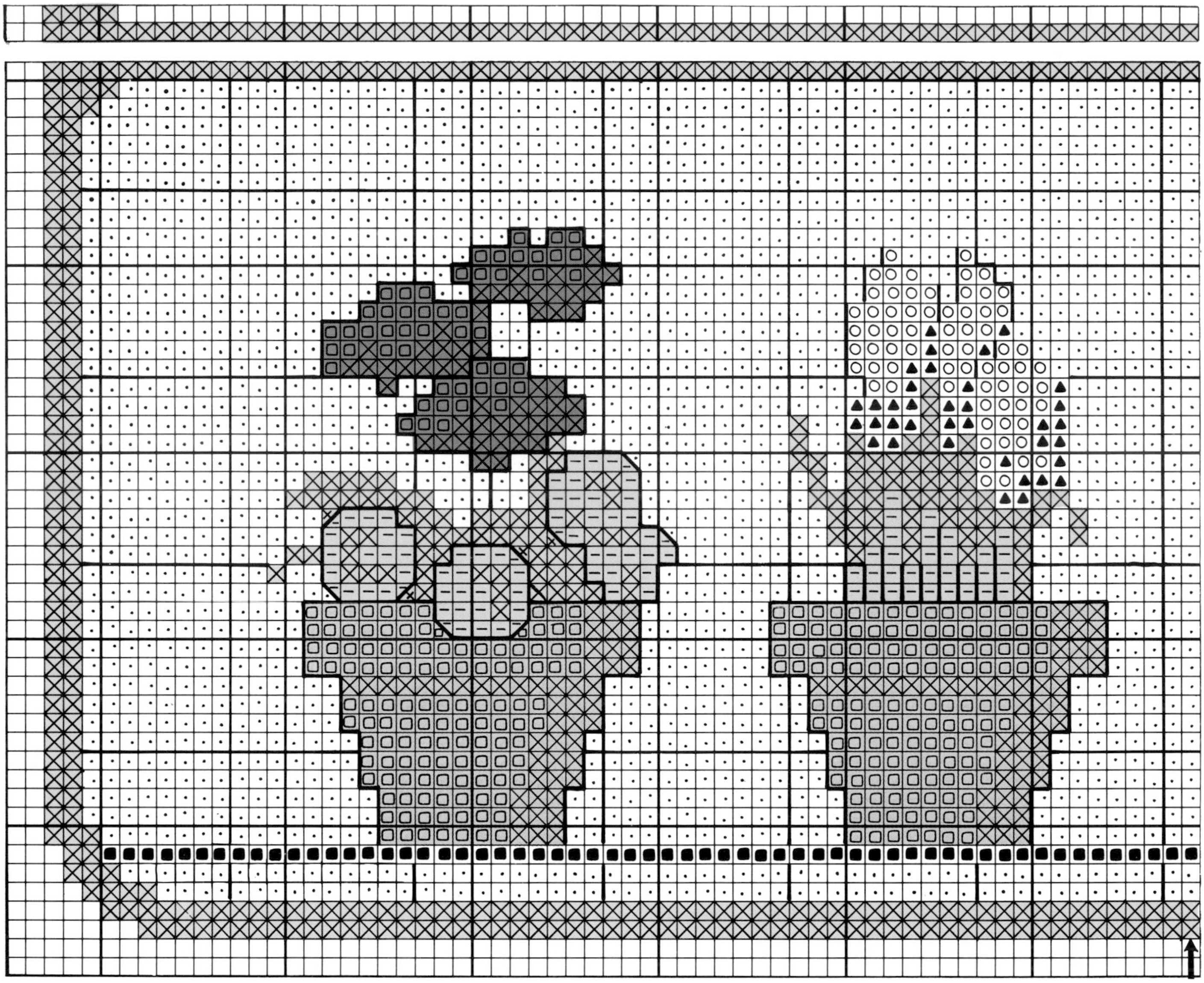

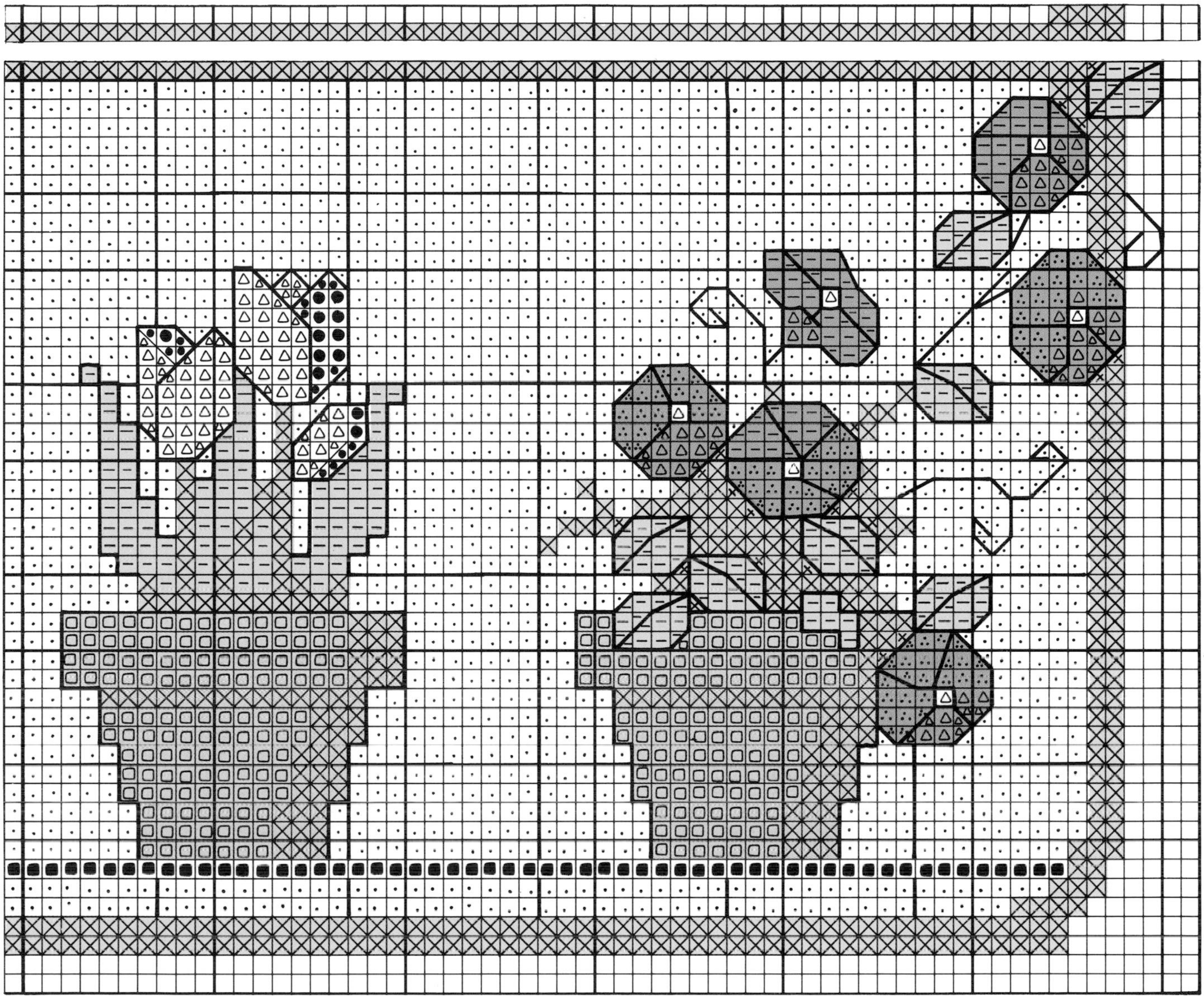

One Summer Afternoon

Stitched on white Belfast Linen 32 over two threads, the finished design size is 7¾" x 12". The fabric was cut 14" x 18".

FABRICS   **DESIGN SIZES**
FABRICS	DESIGN SIZES
Aida 11	11⅛" x 17½"
Aida 14	8¾" x 13¾"
Aida 18	6⅞" x 10⅝"
Hardanger 22	5⅝" x 8¾"

Step One: Cross-stitch (two strands)

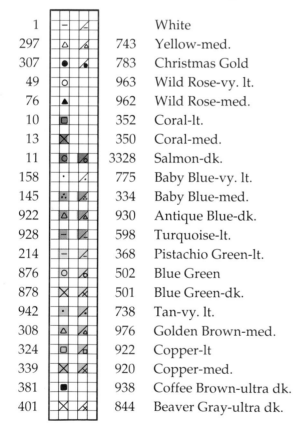

ANCHOR	DMC (used for sample)	
1		White
297	743	Yellow-med.
307	783	Christmas Gold
49	963	Wild Rose-vy. lt.
76	962	Wild Rose-med.
10	352	Coral-lt.
13	350	Coral-med.
11	3328	Salmon-dk.
158	775	Baby Blue-vy. lt.
145	334	Baby Blue-med.
922	930	Antique Blue-dk.
928	598	Turquoise-lt.
214	368	Pistachio Green-lt.
876	502	Blue Green
878	501	Blue Green-dk.
942	738	Tan-vy. lt.
308	976	Golden Brown-med.
324	922	Copper-lt
339	920	Copper-med.
381	938	Coffee Brown-ultra dk.
401	844	Beaver Gray-ultra dk.

Step Two: Backstitch (one strand)

ANCHOR	DMC	
307	783	Christmas Gold (outline of yellow flowers)
76	962	Wild Rose-med. (outline of pink flowers)
11	350	Coral-med. (outline of red flowers)
145	334	Baby Blue-med. (dotted line pattern)
922	930	Antique Blue-dk. (cat's dish, quilt designs in center except houses, blue flowers)
876	502	Blue Green (in word "that" and line under word)
401	844	Beaver Gray-ultra dk. (first and third cats)
339	920	Copper-med. (center cat, houses)
878	501	Blue Green-dk. (all else)

Picture Perfect

The motifs for the wall hanging and frames are from "One Summer Afternoon" (pages 80-86).

The cat design is from the top of the sampler. Stitched on white Belfast Linen 32 over two threads, the finished design size is 8¼" x 6⅛". The stitch count is 131 x 98. The fabric was cut 9" x 10".

The frame design is from the border below the cat design on the sampler. Stitched on white Belfast Linen 32 over two threads, the finished design size is 7½" x 7½". The stitch count is 121 x 121. Begin stitching the original border for the bottom row on the frame. Then repeat the border squares in order up the right side, across the top and down the left side. Opposite borders of the frame should be in reverse order (see photo). The fabric was cut 10" x 10" for each. Stitch two frame pieces.

MATERIALS for wall hanging and frames:
Three completed cross-stitch designs on white Belfast
 Linen 32
Three 8" x 8" pieces of foam board
Five 8" x 8" pieces of poster board
Two 4½" x 4¾" photographs
Three adhesive picture hangers
Glue gun and glue
Pins
Tape

DIRECTIONS:
1. For wall hanging, cut one SEMI-CIRCLE from foam board and one from poster board according to pattern (right). Trim ¼" from all edges of poster board piece. For frames, cut two 7" x 7¼" pieces of foam board and two of poster board. Cut a 4" x 4¼" window in each piece of poster board for mat (Diagram 1). Also cut two 6½" x 6¾" pieces of poster board.

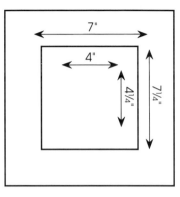

Diagram 1

2. To make wall hanging, trim cat design piece 1½" outside design. Place design piece wrong side up on flat surface. Center semi-circle foam board over design. Wrap fabric to wrong side of foam board, folding corners carefully and dispersing fullness evenly around curved edge. Use pins to temporarily secure fabric, then glue. Center and glue poster board over back of foam board. Let glue dry completely. Attach hanger.

3. To make frame mat, trim one design piece 1½" outside edge of design. Place design piece wrong side up on flat surface. Center poster board mat over design. Trace edge of window onto fabric. Cut opening 1" inside line. Also cut each corner diagonally to line. Fold fabric in window to wrong side of mat. Glue fabric. Center and tape photo behind window.

4. Place mat over foam board. Wrap fabric to wrong side, folding corners carefully. Use pins to temporarily secure fabric, then glue. Center and glue poster board over back of foam board. Attach hanger. Repeat.

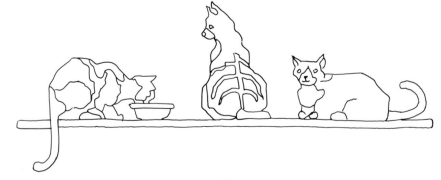

PICTURE PERFECT
SEMI-CIRCLE
Cut 1

Gladness of the heart grows from the wholesome goodness of things homegrown. Surrounded by the sights and smells of golden corn, fresh jam, and homemade cookies just out of the oven, a lingering sense of contentment and well-being feeds the soul.

93

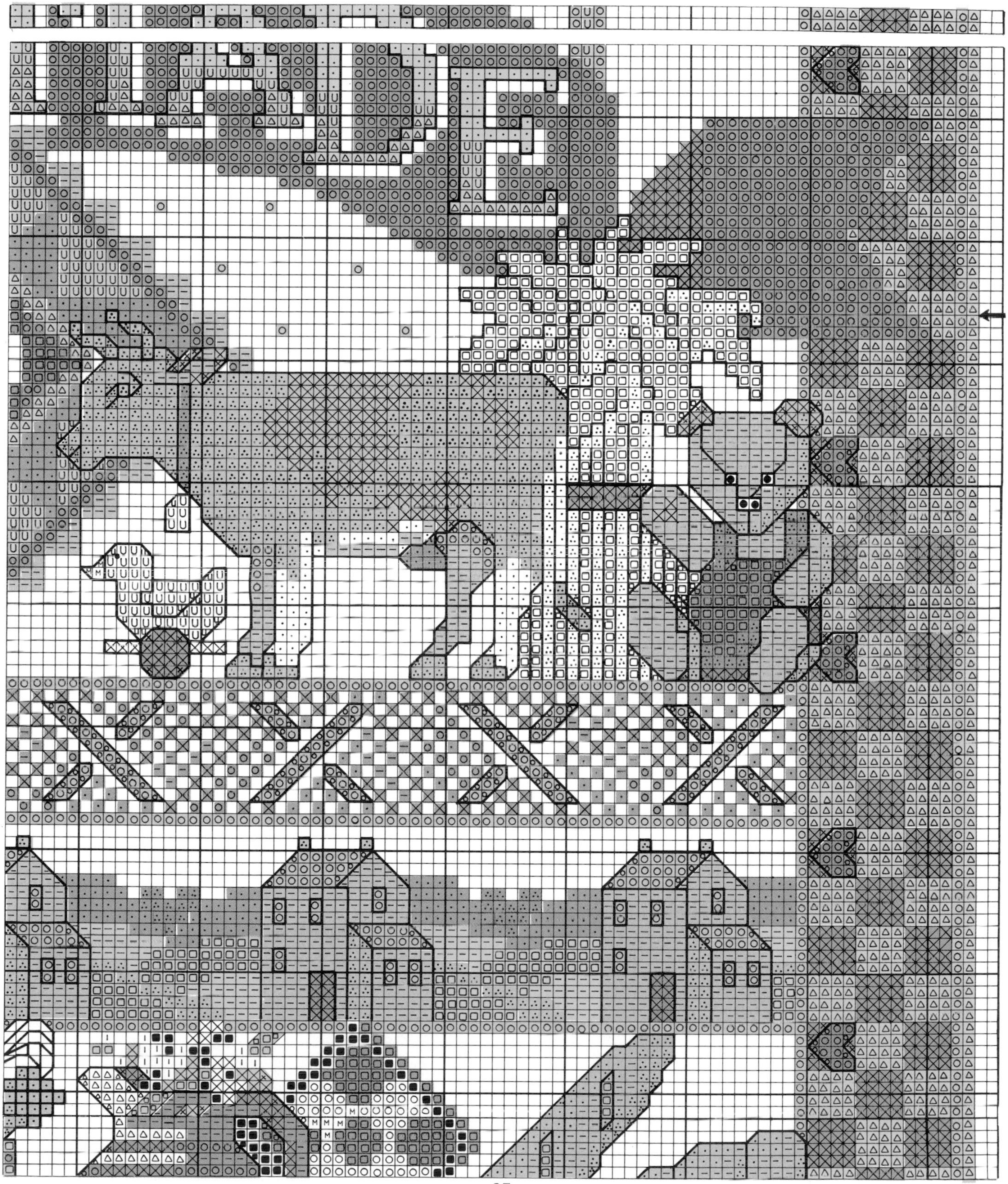

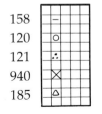

Homemade Hearts

Stitched on brown Perforated Paper 14 over one, the finished design size for the letter "M" is 2½" x 1⅜". The paper was cut 7" x 7" for each letter. Stitch enough letters to complete the word "HOMEMADE." Instructions to complete the project are on page 107.

Step One: Cross-stitch (three strands)

ANCHOR		DMC (used for sample)	
158	–	775	Baby Blue-vy. lt.
120	o	794	Cornflower Blue-lt.
121	∴	793	Cornflower Blue-med.
940	✕	792	Cornflower Blue-dk.
185	△	964	Seagreen-lt.

Step Two: Backstitch (one strand)

940		792	Cornflower Blue-dk. (seagreen hearts)
401		413	Pewter Gray-dk. (letters)

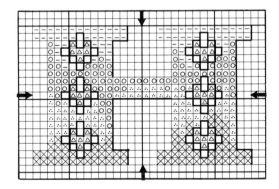

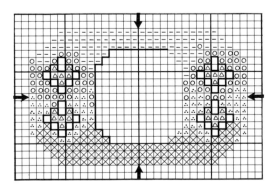

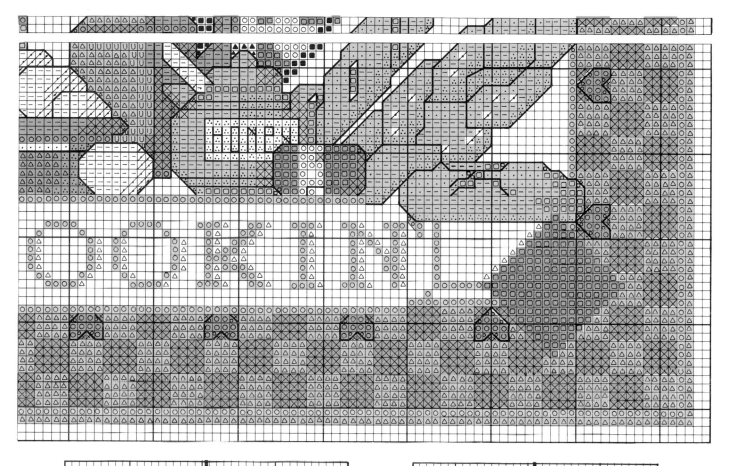

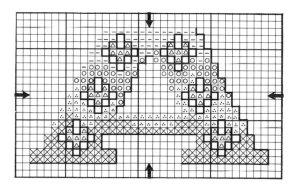

Homegrown Happiness

Stitched on white Belfast Linen 32 over two threads, the finished design size is 10" x 14½". The fabric was cut 16" x 21".

FABRICS	DESIGN SIZES
Aida 11	14½" x 21⅛"
Aida 14	11⅜" x 16⅝"
Aida 18	8⅞" x 12⅞"
Hardanger 22	7¼" x 10½"

Step One: Cross-stitch (two strands)

ANCHOR			DMC	(used for sample)
1				White
387			712	Cream
300			745	Yellow-lt. pale
297			743	Yellow-med.
304			741	Tangerine-med.
316			740	Tangerine
330			947	Burnt Orange
886			677	Old Gold-vy. lt.
891			676	Old Gold-lt.
49			963	Wild Rose-vy. lt.
75			962	Wild Rose-med.
76			961	Wild Rose-dk.
42			309	Rose-deep
47			304	Christmas Red-med.
13			349	Coral-dk.
43			815	Garnet-med.
86			3608	Plum-vy. lt.
87			3607	Plum-lt.
104			210	Lavender-med.
98			553	Violet-med.
870			3042	Antique Violet-lt.
871			3041	Antique Violet-med.
101			327	Antique Violet-vy. dk.
158			775	Baby Blue-vy. lt.
120			794	Cornflower Blue-lt.
121			793	Cornflower Blue-med.
940			792	Cornflower Blue-dk.
941			791	Cornflower Blue-vy. dk.
158			747	Sky Blue-vy. lt.
185			964	Seagreen-lt.
186			959	Seagreen-med.
900			928	Slate Green-lt.
849			927	Slate Green-med.
265			3348	Yellow Green-lt.
242			989	Forest Green
246			986	Forest Green-vy. dk.
215			320	Pistachio Green-med.
216			319	Pistachio Green-vy. dk.
885			739	Tan-ultra vy. lt.
347			402	Mahogany-vy. lt.
324			922	Copper-lt.
349			301	Mahogany-med.
351			400	Mahogany-dk.
352			300	Mahogany-vy. dk.
381			938	Coffee Brown-ultra dk.
830			644	Beige Gray-med.
392			642	Beige Gray-dk.
903			640	Beige Gray-vy. dk.
398			415	Pearl Gray
400			414	Steel Gray-dk.
236			3799	Pewter Gray-vy. dk.
403			310	Black

Step Two: Backstitch (one strand)

43		815	Garnet-med. (hearts in border)
941		791	Cornflower Blue-vy. dk. (jam jar, "JAM," tablecloth, egg bowl, cannister, pitcher, duck wheels, "HOMEMADE," grapes)
216		319	Pistachio Green-vy. dk. (corn husks, pear leaves, apple leaves, grape leaves)
309		435	Brown-vy. lt. (eggs, wheat stocks, wheat kernels, corn)
349		301	Mahogany-med. (ducks)
352		300	Mahogany-vy. dk. (bread, honey, "HONEY," rolling pin, cherry pie, spoon, meat tenderizer, teddy bears, cows, banana stems, cornucopia, cow's eyes, grape stem)
381		938	Coffee Brown-ultra dk. (Xs in border)
400		414	Steel Gray-dk. (around milk bottle)
236		3799	Pewter Gray-vy. dk. (flour sack, cow's horns, whisk "FLOUR," "MI" of Milk)
403		310	Black (houses, bear's eyes and nose, cherry stems, watermelon seeds)

Step Three: French Knots (one strand)

349		301	Mahogany-med.

98

The Pantry Maid

The designs for the dress are from "Homegrown Happiness" (pages 92-97). The design strips are composed from elements of the sampler; choose motifs as desired. Stitch a total of 11 design strips from cream Belfast Linen 32, raw linen Belfast Linen 32, and Quaker Cloth 28. Each design area should be 6"-8" long. See photo for ideas.

MATERIALS for doll body:
½ yard of muslin; matching thread
Assorted dry pasta for hair
Stuffing
Glue gun and glue
10" of a ¼"-wide dowel
Two small snap sets

DIRECTIONS:
1. Cut doll BODY, ARMs, LEGs and SOLEs from muslin according to patterns (pages 102-105).

2. Stitch two leg pieces together on front and back edges. Stitch sole to bottom of leg. Turn. Stuff firmly to within ¾" of top edge. Repeat.

3. Stitch two arm pieces together, leaving an opening; see pattern. Turn. Repeat.

4. Stitch darts in body pieces. Stitch arms to body, still leaving an opening in arm seam. Then stitch body pieces together, leaving bottom edge open. Position doll leg with front and back seams matching. Place on bottom edge of doll front with raw edges matching; see pattern. Stitch. Turn. Stuff arms through opening in seam. Slipstitch opening closed. Stuff top of head firmly. Insert dowel in body. Stuff body firmly. Slipstitch opening closed at doll bottom.

5. To form fingers, longstitch from front to back through points as indicated on pattern. Glue dry pasta to head of doll as desired after dressing her (see photo).

MATERIALS for dress and boots:
¼ yard of each of the following (includes completed cross-stitch designs): cream Belfast Linen 32, Quaker Cloth 32, and raw linen Belfast Linen 32
1½ yards of muslin; matching thread
⅛ yard of black linen; matching thread
⅛ yard of black fabric
Eight small black buttons
½ yard of ⅛"-wide elastic
One pair of light blue stretch lace baby socks

DIRECTIONS:
1. Trace BODICE FRONT, BODICE BACK and SLEEVE patterns (pages 102-103) onto muslin, allowing 1" between pieces. Cut general shapes about ½" outside lines. Also cut one 11½" x 41" piece for skirt.

2. From raw Belfast linen, cut 2"-wide bias, piecing as needed to equal 60". Set aside.

3. Cut some small, unevenly shaped triangles and strips from remainder of each of the three design fabrics. Place one piece of unstitched design fabric on one bodice back muslin piece. Pin second unstitched design fabric piece over first, aligning one edge; stitch through all layers (Diagram 1). Trim seam allowance

(continued on page 101)

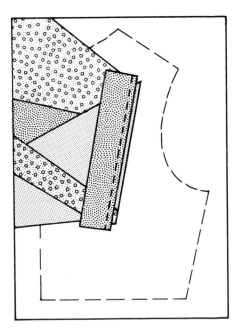

Diagram 1

to ¼" if necessary. Fold second piece open and press flat. Place third piece over existing pieces at random. Continue to stitch and unfold, pressing frequently, until all of bodice back area is covered. Repeat for second bodice back piece.

4. Plan placement for design pieces on bodice front, sleeves and skirt. Mark on muslin. (The model has three design pieces on the bodice front, the skirt and one sleeve. The second sleeve has two pieces.) Piece unstitched design fabric pieces and design pieces at random, working from placement of design pieces.

5. Place patterns over joined pieces and check placement of designs. Cut out all bodice and sleeve pieces. Trim skirt piece to 10½" x 40".

6. Stitch bodice front to bodice back at shoulders. Stitch gathering threads in sleeve cap. Gather sleeve to fit armhole; stitch to bodice. Repeat with second sleeve. Stitch gathering threads in wrist of sleeve. Gather to 4". From bias strips, cut one 4" piece. Stitch bias to sleeve at wrist with right sides together. Repeat. Fold bodice and sleeves with right sides together. Stitch side seams and sleeves through bias. Fold bias double to wrong side and slipstitch.

7. Fold one center back seam under ¼" and slipstitch narrow hem. Cut one 8" piece of bias. Stitch to neck of dress with right sides together. Fold double to the wrong side and slipstitch.

8. Cut one 40" piece of bias. Stitch to bottom edge of skirt piece with right sides together. Stitch short ends of skirt piece with right sides together to within 1" of waist edge. Fold bias double to the wrong side and slipstitch. Mark center of waist edges of skirt and bodice. Stitch gathering threads on waist edge of skirt. Gather skirt to fit bodice. Match centers of bodice and skirt; stitch. Sew snaps to center back opening at neck and waist of dress.

9. To make bloomers, cut BLOOMER pieces from muslin according to pattern (page 105). Stitch center front and back seams with right sides together. Fold, aligning center seams. Then stitch the inseam.

10. Fold waist edge ½" double to the wrong side to make casing. Stitch, leaving an opening. Thread elastic through casing. Overlap ends of elastic ½" and secure. Stitch opening closed.

11. Stitch a narrow hem in each leg. Sew elastic thread ½" above hem, either by hand or with zigzag stitch over elastic. Gather to fit doll and secure.

12. To make boots, cut BOOT, FLAP and SOLE pieces from black linen according to patterns (page 106). Also cut boot and boot flap pieces from black fabric for lining.

13. Stitch boot flap and boot flap lining together on top, scalloped and bottom edges with right sides together. Clip seam allowances; turn and press. Place top of boot flap ¼" below top edge of one boot side piece with right sides together. Stitch. Stitch two boot side pieces with right sides together on heel seam. Stitch two boot lining pieces with right sides together on heel seam. Match heel seams of boot and boot lining with right sides together and stitch top of boot. Turn. Fold in half to form boot, and stitch from top of boot to bottom of toe, stitching through all layers. Proceed to treat boot and lining as one piece of fabric. Stitch sole to bottom of boot. Clip corners. Turn. Repeat for other boot, reversing position of flap.

14. Fold flap over side of boot. Sew buttons on scallops. Repeat. Place socks and boots on doll.

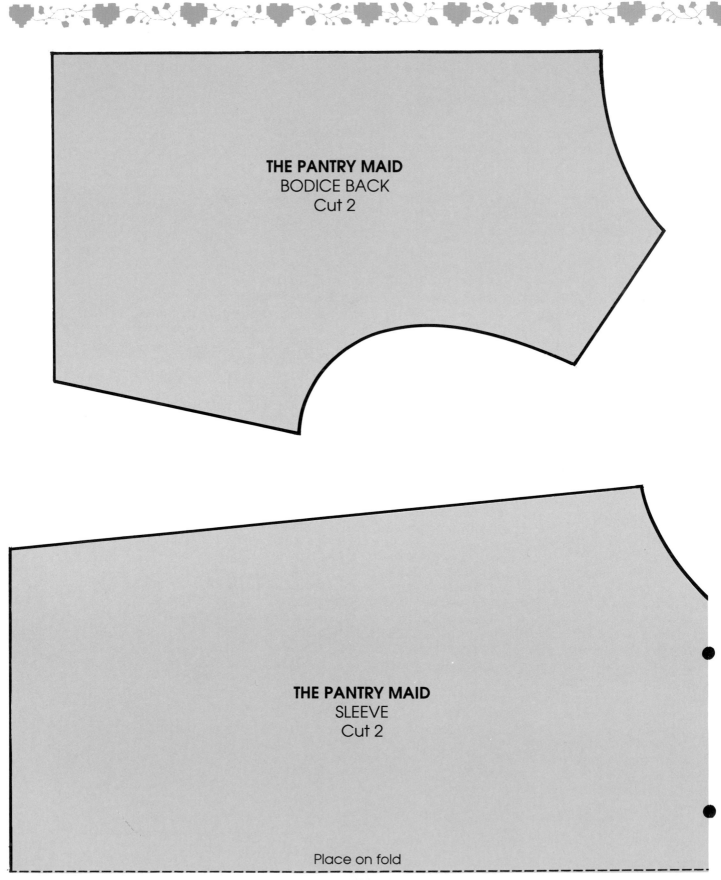

THE PANTRY MAID
BODICE BACK
Cut 2

THE PANTRY MAID
SLEEVE
Cut 2

Place on fold

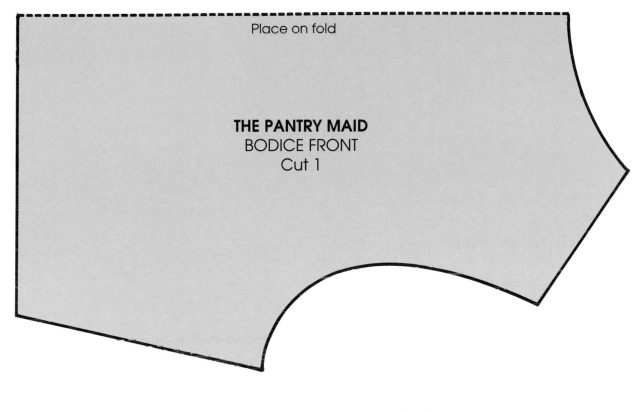

Place on fold

THE PANTRY MAID
BODICE FRONT
Cut 1

Match patterns
at each ●

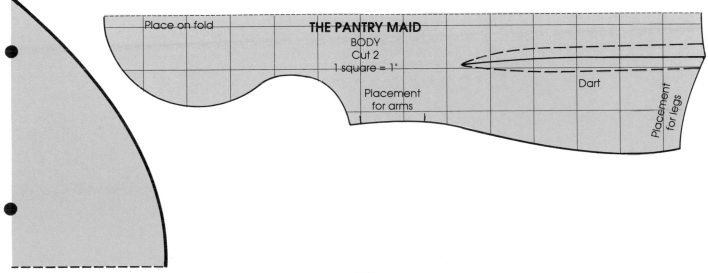

Place on fold

THE PANTRY MAID
BODY
Cut 2
1 square = 1"

Placement
for arms

Dart

Placement
for legs

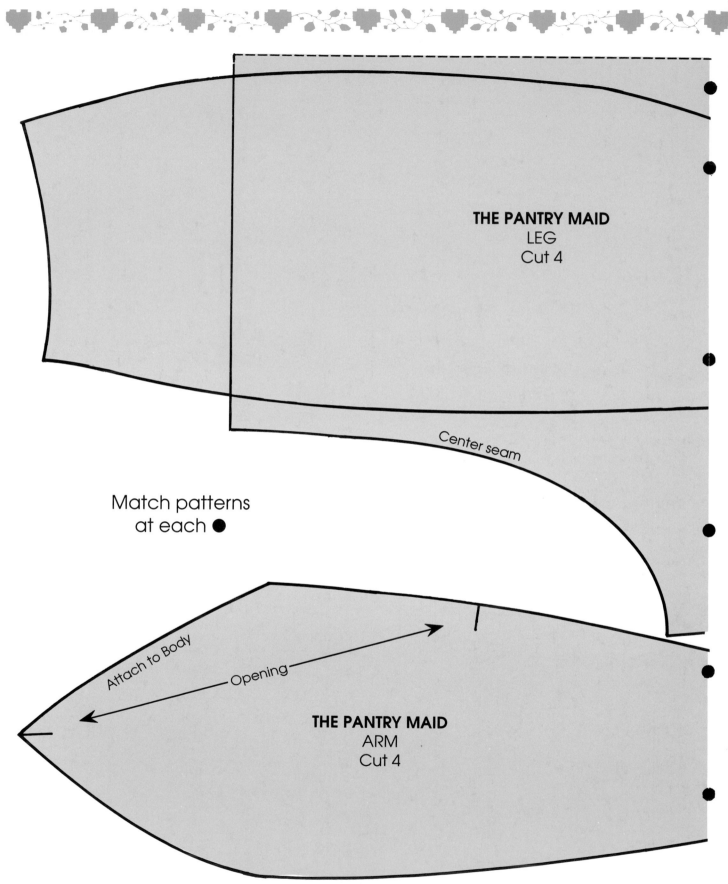

THE PANTRY MAID
LEG
Cut 4

Center seam

Match patterns
at each ●

Attach to Body

Opening

THE PANTRY MAID
ARM
Cut 4

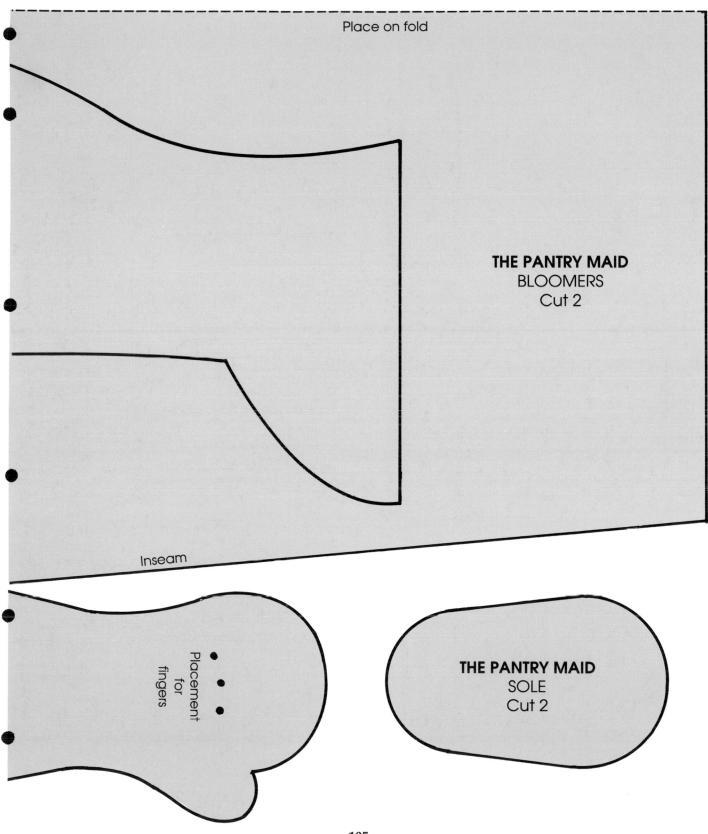

Place on fold

THE PANTRY MAID
BLOOMERS
Cut 2

Inseam

Placement
for
fingers

THE PANTRY MAID
SOLE
Cut 2

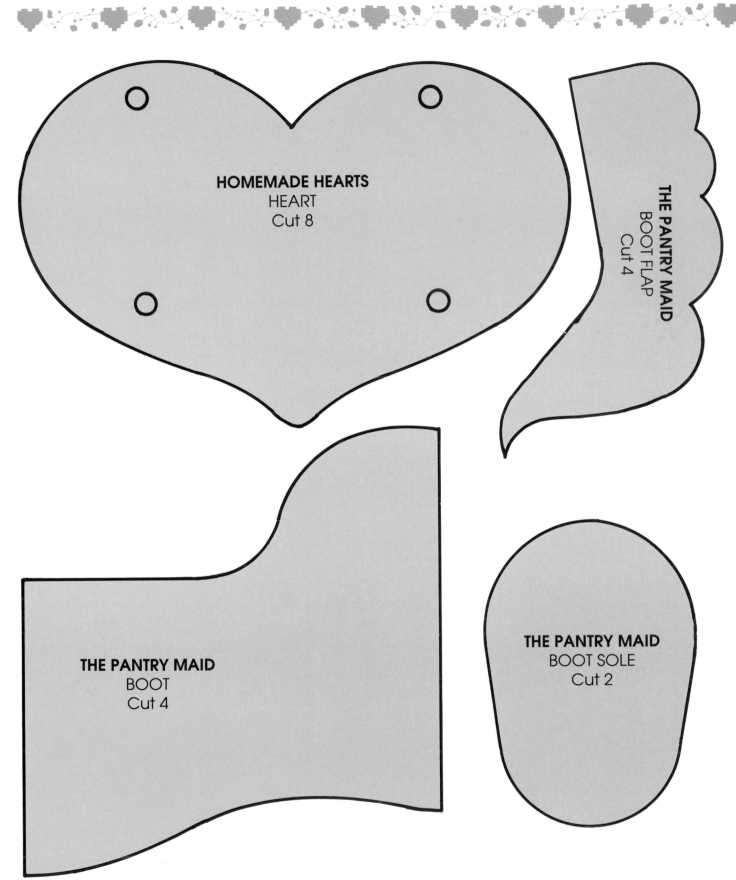

HOMEMADE HEARTS
HEART
Cut 8

THE PANTRY MAID
BOOT FLAP
Cut 4

THE PANTRY MAID
BOOT
Cut 4

THE PANTRY MAID
BOOT SOLE
Cut 2

Homemade Hearts

MATERIALS:
Eight completed cross-stitch designs on brown
Perforated Paper 14 (code and graphs on pages 96-
97)
3 feet of 6"-wide ¼" double-face finished plywood
1¾ yards of ¼"-wide brown satin cording
Drill and ¼" drill bit
Brown paint
Spray adhesive

DIRECTIONS:
1. From plywood, cut eight HEARTs (including holes)
according to pattern (left). On one heart, cut only top
holes. This will be used for the last letter in the chain
(see photo). Paint the front and back of hearts. Set
aside and let dry completely.

2. Trace pattern onto design pieces with letters
centered and marking placement for holes. Cut out
design pieces (including holes) according to pattern.
On one "E" design, cut only top holes. (This will be the
last letter in the chain.) Glue one design piece to each
heart matching holes.

3. Leaving a 6"-deep loop at the top, string the ends of
the cording through the top holes of the first "H" from
front to back. String the ends through the bottom holes
from back to front. Repeat with the remaining seven
hearts to spell "HOMEMADE." Pull the cording taut
so that the tops and bottoms of the hearts touch. Tie
ends of cording in a knot behind final "E" and trim
ends.

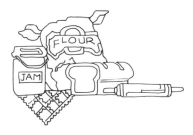

107

The nostalgia of an old-time Christmas beckons across the miles. On city streets and country roads, travelers burst through the doors of condos and cottages, arms brimming with festive packages for one and all.

Christmas Homecoming

Stitched on dirty linen Dublin Linen 25 over two threads, the finished design size is 17¼" x 12¾". The fabric was cut 24" x 19". (This code is also used for the "Heart Ornaments" graph below and on page 117, and for the "Christmas Card Box" graph on page 121.)

FABRICS
Aida 11
Aida 14
Aida 18
Hardanger 22

DESIGN SIZES
19½" x 14½"
15⅜" x 11⅜"
12" x 8⅞"
9¾" x 7¼"

Step One: Cross-stitch (two strands)

ANCHOR		DMC (used for sample)	
1			White
300		745	Yellow-lt. pale
297		743	Yellow-med.
4146		754	Peach-lt.
8		353	Peach
26		3708	Melon-lt.
27		893	Carnation-lt.
35		891	Carnation-dk.
59		326	Rose-vy. deep

158		775	Baby Blue-lt.
130		809	Delft
131		798	Delft-dk.
186		959	Seagreen-med.
187		958	Seagreen-dk.
206		955	Nile Green-lt.
209		913	Nile Green-med.
210		562	Jade-med.
189		991	Aquamarine-dk.
349		301	Mahogany-med.
357		801	Coffee Brown-dk.

Step Two: Backstitch (one strand)

59		326	Rose-vy. deep (hearts)
130		809	Delft (angel wings)
189		991	Aquamarine-dk. (trees, man's shirt)
879		500	Blue Green-vy. dk. (words)
357		801	Coffee Brown-dk. (all else)

This graph is for the "Heart Ornaments" (page 119). The graph continues on page 117. Use the codes on this page.

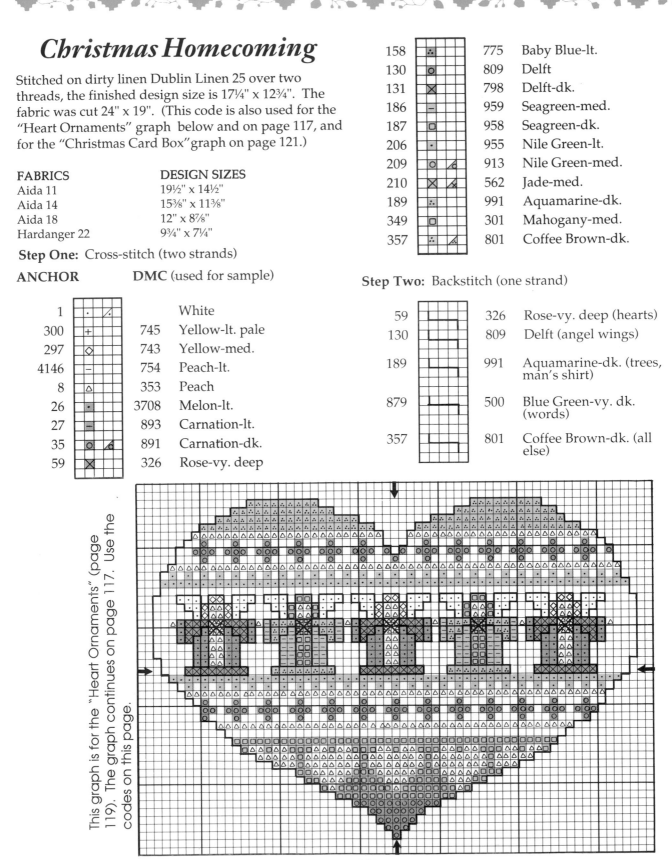

110

Stitch Count: 215 x 159

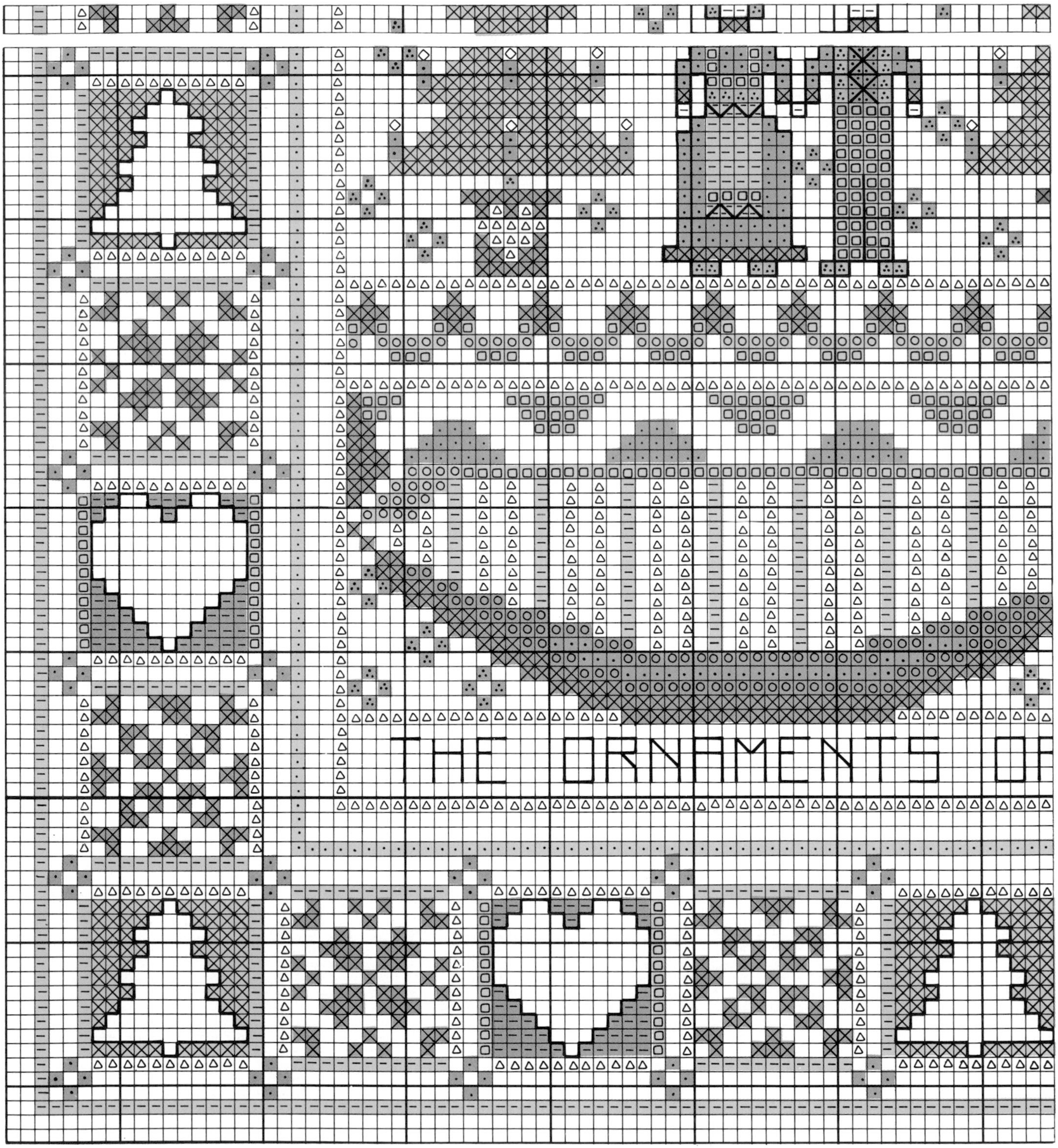
THE ORNAMENTS OF

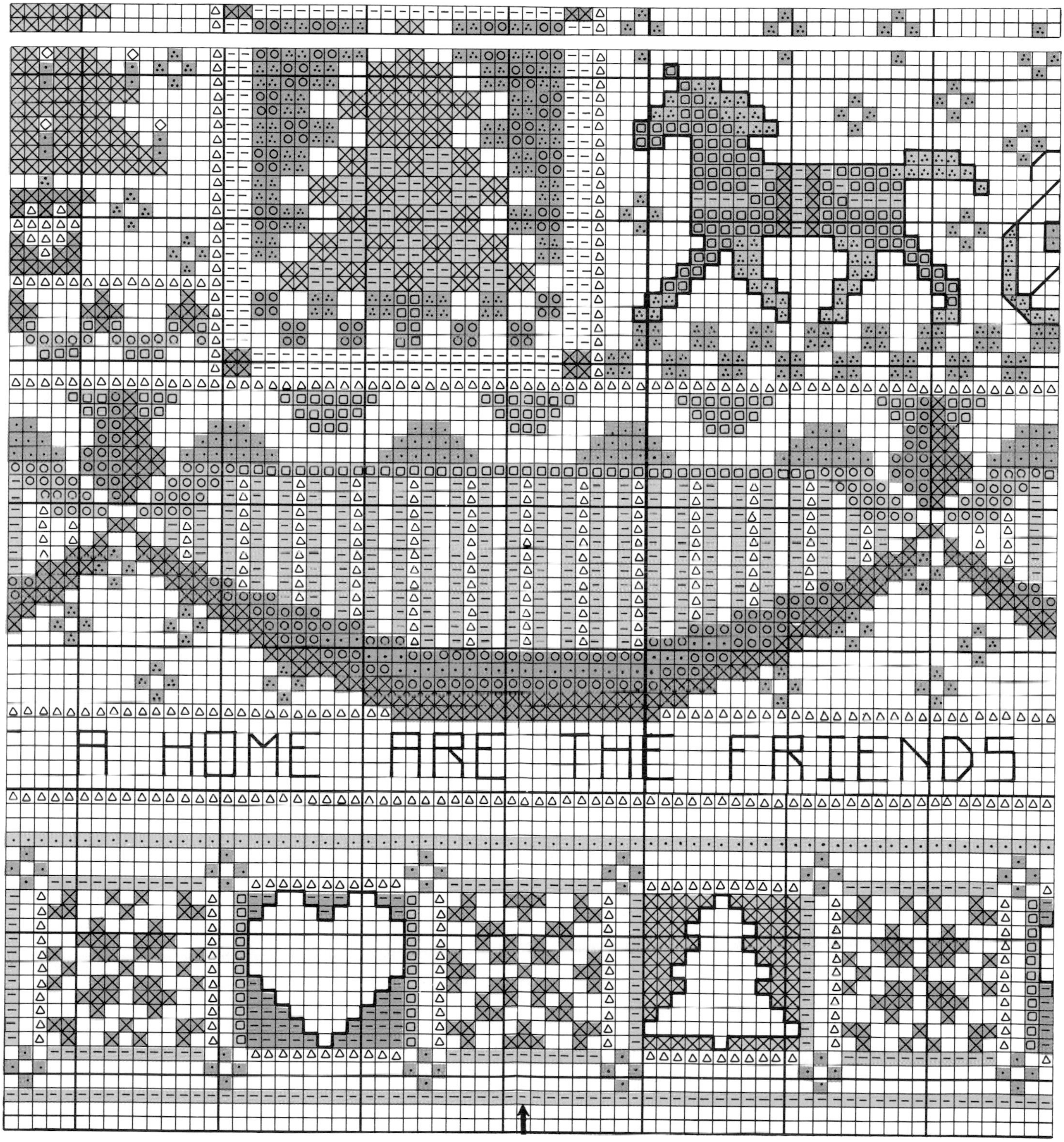
A HOME ARE THE FRIENDS

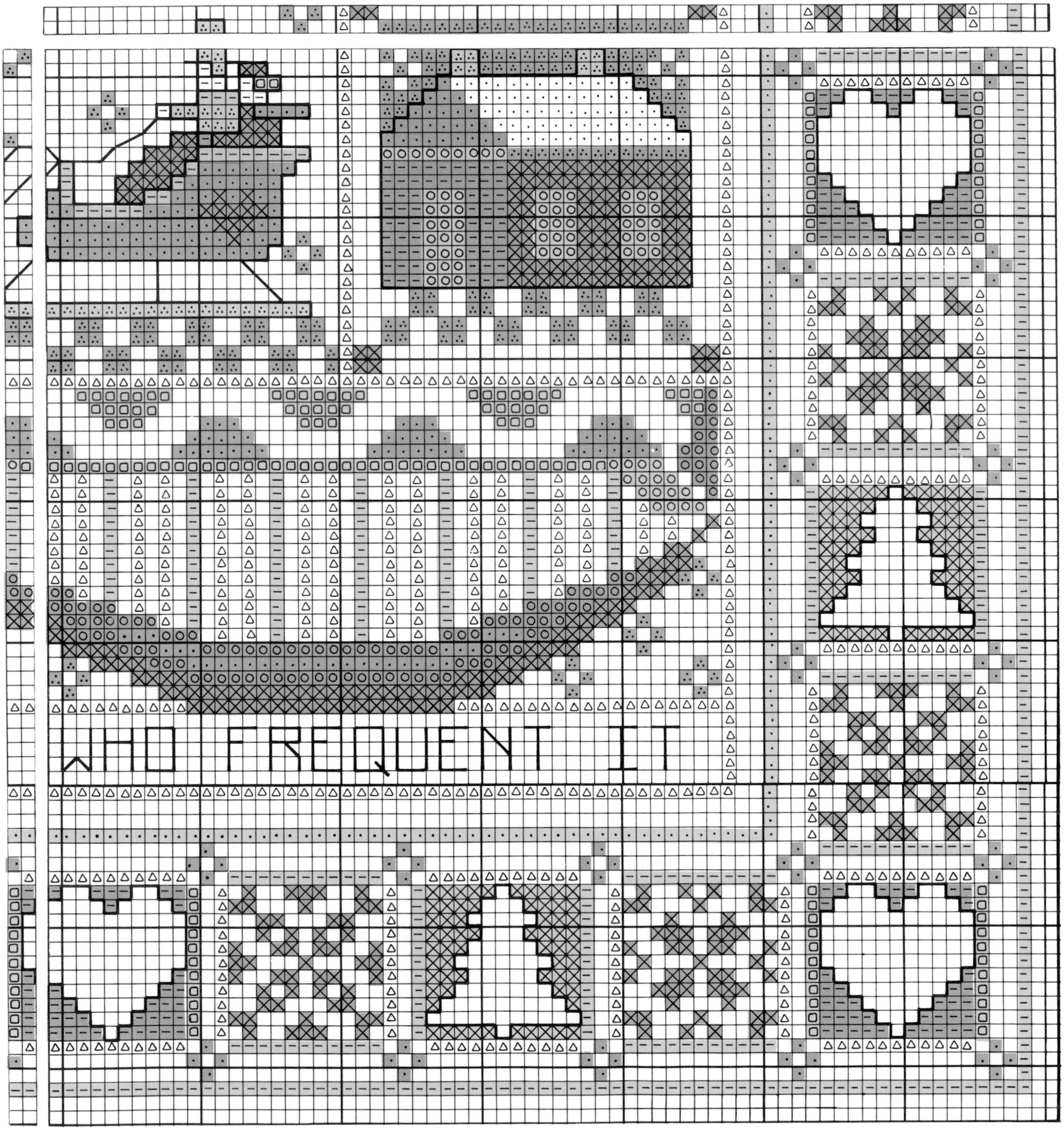
WHO FREQUENT IT

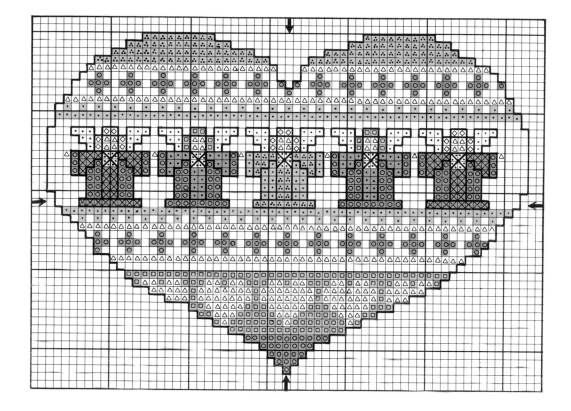

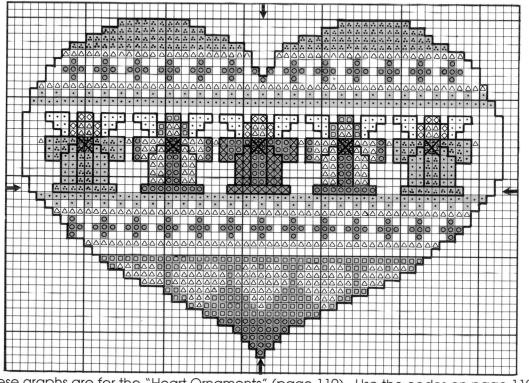

These graphs are for the "Heart Ornaments" (page 119). Use the codes on page 110.

Heart Ornaments

The designs for the hearts are from the graphs on pages 110 and 117. Use the code for "Christmas Homecoming" (page 110). Stitched on dirty linen Dublin Linen 25 over two threads, the finished design size for one heart is 4⅞" x 3½". The stitch count is 61 x 43. The fabric was cut 7" x 5" for each heart.

MATERIALS for one:
Completed cross-stitched design on dirty
    linen Dublin Linen 25; matching thread
One 6" x 4" piece of unstitched raw linen
    Dublin Linen 25
⅝ yard of ⅛"-wide rayon trim
Stuffing

DIRECTIONS:
1. Cut design piece ¼" outside stitching. Cut one heart from unstitched linen for back according to design piece.

2. Stitch design piece to back with right sides together, leaving an opening. Turn. Stuff moderately. Slipstitch opening closed.

3. Whipstitch trim around heart on the seam, beginning and ending at center top of heart. Make a 2½"-deep loop for hanger with remaining trim. Whipstitch ends of hanger on back of ornament.

Wreath Ornaments

The motifs for the "Wreath Ornaments" are from "Christmas Homecoming" (pages 110-16). All ornaments are stitched on raw linen Dublin Linen 25 over two threads.

Sleigh: The finished design size is 4½" x 2¼". The stitch count is 56 x 28. The fabric was cut 9" x 7".

Sheep: The finished design size is 3⅜" x 1½". The stitch count is 42 x 19. The fabric was cut 8" x 6".

House: The finished design size is 2¼" x 2¼". The stitch count is 28 x 28. The fabric was cut 6" x 6".

Single tree: The finished design size is 2¼" x 2¼". The stitch count is 28 x 28. The fabric was cut 6" x 6".

Four-tree square: The finished design size is 4⅛" x 4⅛". The stitch count is 52 x 52. The fabric was cut 9" x 9".

Star square: The finished design size is 3½" x 3½". The stitch count is 44 x 44. The fabric was cut 8" x 8".

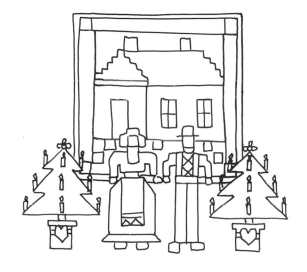

(continued on next page)

MATERIALS for one Wreath Ornament:
Completed cross-stitch design on dirty linen Dublin
   Linen 25; matching thread
Scrap of unstitched raw linen Dublin Linen 25 for back
Stuffing
Assorted beads, trims and cording

DIRECTIONS:
1. Cut design piece ¼" outside stitching. Cut a
matching piece of unstitched linen for back. Stitch
design piece to back with right sides together, leaving

an opening. Turn. Stuff firmly. Slipstitch opening
closed.

2. Adorn ornament with beads, cording and other
trims as desired (see photo). Make a loop from a piece
of trim for hanging and tack to back of ornament.

Note: To make the wreath, tack the ornaments to
various lengths of cording and beaded strings. Tie all
lengths together in a loop at the top, letting the
ornaments hang as desired.

Christmas Card Box

Back: The design for the back is from "Christmas
Homecoming" (pages 110-116). The motif is the man
and woman holding hands, with an evergreen on each
side of them, located in the lower middle of the graph.
Stitched on brown Perforated Paper 14 over one, the
finished design size is 4⅝" x 2⅜". The stitch count is 64
x 33. The paper was cut 12" x 12". See Step 2 of
instructions before stitching.

Front: The design for the front is from "Christmas
Homecoming" and the graph on the next page. Use
the code for "Christmas Homecoming" (page 110).
Stitched on brown Perforated Paper 14 over one, the
finished design size is 12⅜" x 2⅞". The paper was cut
16" x 7". The graph on the next page is for the left and
right sides of the design. Begin stitching the woman/
man and evergreen motifs from "Christmas
Homecoming" (pages 110-116) between the heavy
lines on the graph (next page). The complete design
should be in this order: man, tree, woman/man, tree,
woman/man, tree, woman/man, tree, woman (see
photo).

MATERIALS:
Two completed cross-stitch designs on brown
   Perforated Paper 14
Two 18" x 12" pieces of unstitched brown Perforated
   Paper 14
One 20" x 14" piece of ¼" Masonite
Two yards of ⅜"-wide dark green twisted satin
   cording
Spray adhesive
Wood glue
Glue gun and glue
Craft knife

DIRECTIONS:
1. Cut one BACK piece from Masonite according to
pattern (page 123). From Masonite, cut two 3" squares
for sides, one 11⅞" x 3" piece for bottom and one 12½"
x 3" for front. From perforated paper, cut two 3½" x 3"
pieces for sides.

2. Glue back design piece to smooth side of Masonite back with spray adhesive centering top of design ⅜" from top. Trim perforated paper with a knife working from the back side. Set aside.

3. Glue Masonite side pieces to bottom piece with wood glue. Then glue front to bottom/side pieces to make holder (Diagram 1).

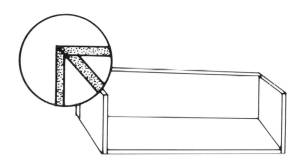

Diagram 1

4. With spray adhesive, glue front design piece to Masonite centering design. Trim edge of perforated paper with knife working from the back side. Glue one perforated paper side piece to the smooth side of one Masonite side piece with spray adhesive matching edges. Repeat with other side piece.

5. Glue Masonite holder to back piece with wood glue so that all edges align.

6. Knot one end of cording. Beginning at top edge of right side piece, glue knotted end with hot glue leaving a 3" tail. Continue gluing cording around top of back piece and holder ending at right side and leaving a 4" tail; knot end. Make a bow with remaining cording. Glue where the two tails meet (see photo).

Left   Right

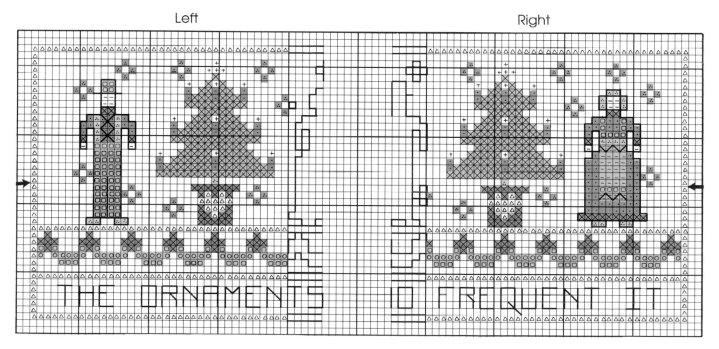

Use the code from "Christmas Homecoming" (page 110)

Christmas Tree Ball

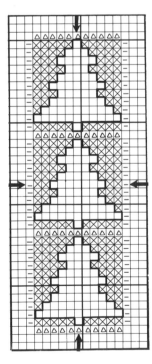

Stitched on raw linen Dublin Linen 25 over two threads, the finished design size is 1" x 3". The stitch count is 13 x 37. The fabric was cut 7" x 9". Trace four SECTION patterns on unstitched linen before stitching. Begin stitching in center of each section.

Step One: Cross-stitch (two strands)

ANCHOR		DMC (used for sample)	
8	△	353	Peach
186	-	959	Seagreen-med.
210	✕	562	Jade-med.

Step Two: Backstitch (one strand)

189		991	Aquamarine-dk.

MATERIALS:
Four completed cross-stitch designs on raw linen
    Dublin Linen 25
1½ yards of ⅞"-wide trim
One 4" Styrofoam ball
One purchased glass ornament
Cold glue gun and glue
Craft knife

DIRECTIONS:
1. Cut out design pieces.

2. Mark the center top and center bottom of the Styrofoam ball. Draw vertical pencil lines around ball to divide it into four equal quarters. Score lines with paring knife. Center and pin design pieces over Styrofoam ball. Poke fabric into Styrofoam ball on score lines, taking small tucks as needed to mold fabric over round surface. Keep score lines as narrow and inconspicuous as possible. Trim excess fabric from edges.

3. Cut two 50" pieces of the trim. Center and glue trim over score lines, leaving two 3¼"-deep loops at bottom end of ornament. Cut a 3" piece of trim for a hanger. Make a bow with remaining trim and glue to top end of ornament. From 3" piece of trim, make a 1½"-deep loop for hanger. Glue hanger to center of bow.

4. Attach purchased ornament on loops at bottom of ornament (see photo).

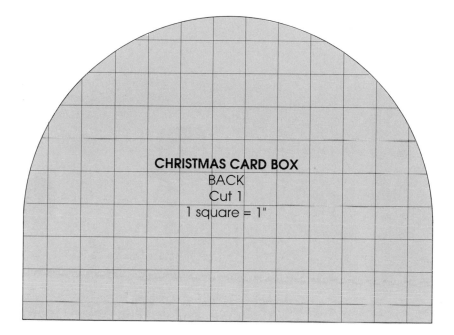

CHRISTMAS CARD BOX
BACK
Cut 1
1 square = 1"

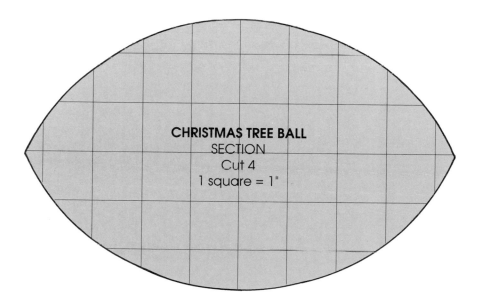

CHRISTMAS TREE BALL
SECTION
Cut 4
1 square = 1"

A special wardrobe for Elizabeth will keep her dressed in style through a year of changing seasons and holiday celebrations.

Doll Body

MATERIALS:
Porcelain doll parts (see Suppliers)
⅛ yard of white fabric; matching thread
Stuffing
Glue

DIRECTIONS:
All seam allowances are ¼"

1. Cut all DOLL BODY pieces from white fabric according to patterns.

2. With right sides together, fold one arm piece in half to equal 1⅜" wide. Stitch the long seam only; do not turn. Position porcelain arm with hand down and insert into fabric arm. With side seam aligned with porcelain underarm, and ¼" of fabric above groove on the upper porcelain arm, secure the fabric to the porcelain by tying thread tightly around the groove. Glue the fabric to the porcelain above the groove (Diagram 1). Pull the hand through and turn fabric. Stuff fabric portion of arm. Slipstitch opening closed. Repeat for second arm.

3. To make legs, fold one leg piece in half to equal 1¾" at top. Stitch the long seam only; do not turn. Repeat Step 2 with fabric legs and porcelain feet, aligning back seam of fabric with back of porcelain leg.

4. Sew darts in the body pieces. With the heel placed on the right side of the back piece, align the raw edges of one upper leg with the bottom raw edges of the back piece; stitch (Diagram 2). Repeat for second leg. With right sides together, and with legs still inside body pieces, stitch front and back together, leaving a 1¾" opening at the top. Pull legs through and turn fabric. Stuff firmly; slipstitch top opening closed. Tack arms to top of body ¾" apart. Glue porcelain head to top of body over arms.

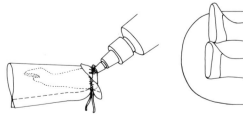

Diagram 1   *Diagram 2*

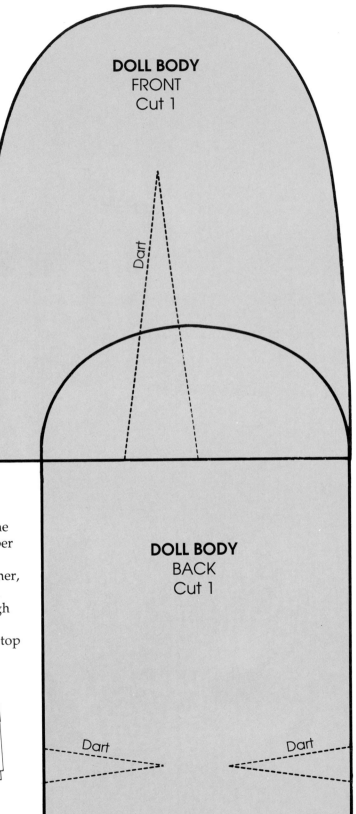

DOLL BODY
FRONT
Cut 1

Dart

DOLL BODY
BACK
Cut 1

Dart   Dart

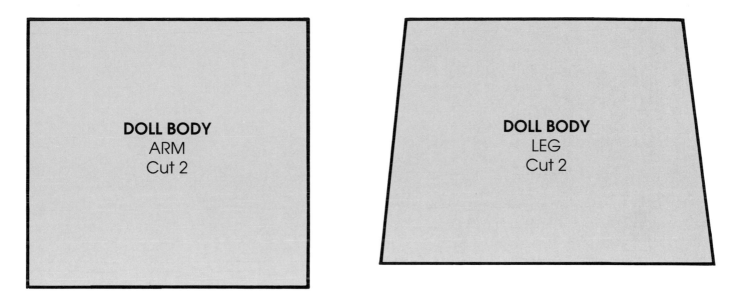

DOLL BODY
ARM
Cut 2

DOLL BODY
LEG
Cut 2

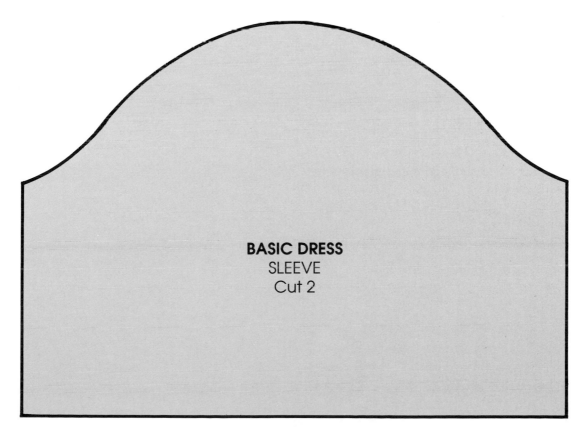

BASIC DRESS
SLEEVE
Cut 2

Basic Dress

MATERIALS:
¼ yard of 45"-wide fabric; matching thread
Two small snaps
6"-8" of elastic thread

DIRECTIONS:
All seam allowances are ¼".

1. Cut one 24" x 6½" piece for the skirt. Then cut out all BASIC DRESS pieces according to patterns (pages 127 and 129).

2. With right sides of one bodice front and two bodice back pieces together, stitch the shoulders. Repeat for lining.

3. Place right sides of the bodice and bodice lining together, matching shoulder seams. Stitch along one center back seam, around the neck, and the second center back. Clip the curved edges. Turn right side out. Proceed to treat both layers of the bodice as one layer of fabric.

4. Stitch a ⅛"-wide hem in the wrist edge of one sleeve. Stitch gathering threads in sleeve cap. Gather the sleeve to fit the armhole. Stitch the sleeve cap to the bodice. Repeat.

5. Sew elastic thread ¼" above the hem at the wrist, either by hand or with a zigzag stitch. With right sides together, stitch one bodice side seam and one sleeve. Repeat for the remaining side seam and sleeve.

6. Fold the skirt with right sides together to equal 12" wide. Stitch the short ends to within 2" of the top edge; backstitch. Press seam open. (This seam is the center back; the long edge with the opening will be the waist.)

7. Mark the center front of the skirt at the waist. Stitch gathering threads along the waist. Fold ½" hem double to the wrong side along the lower edge of the skirt. Hem by hand or machine.

8. Mark the center front of the bodice at the waist. Gather the skirt to fit the bodice. With right sides together, match the center of the skirt to the center of the bodice and stitch. Sew snaps on the center back opening at the neck and waist of the dress.

Pantaloons

MATERIALS:
⅛ yard of lightweight fabric; matching thread
3" of ⅛"-wide elastic
6"-8" of elastic thread

DIRECTIONS:
All seam allowances are ¼".

1. Cut PANTALOONS pieces according to pattern.

2. With right sides together, stitch the front to back along center seams. Stitch a narrow hem in the bottom of each leg. Sew elastic thread ½" above hem, either by hand or with a zigzag stitch. Fold, aligning center seams. Then stitch the inseam.

3. Fold waist edge ½" double to the wrong side to make casing. Thread elastic through casing; overlap ends ½" and secure. Stitch opening closed.

Note: The pantaloons for the "Shamrock Frock" are made from light green fabric. The pantaloons for "Whispers of Spring" are made from cream fabric. The pantaloons for "The Cat's Meow" are made from white fabric and trimmed with lace at the ankles.

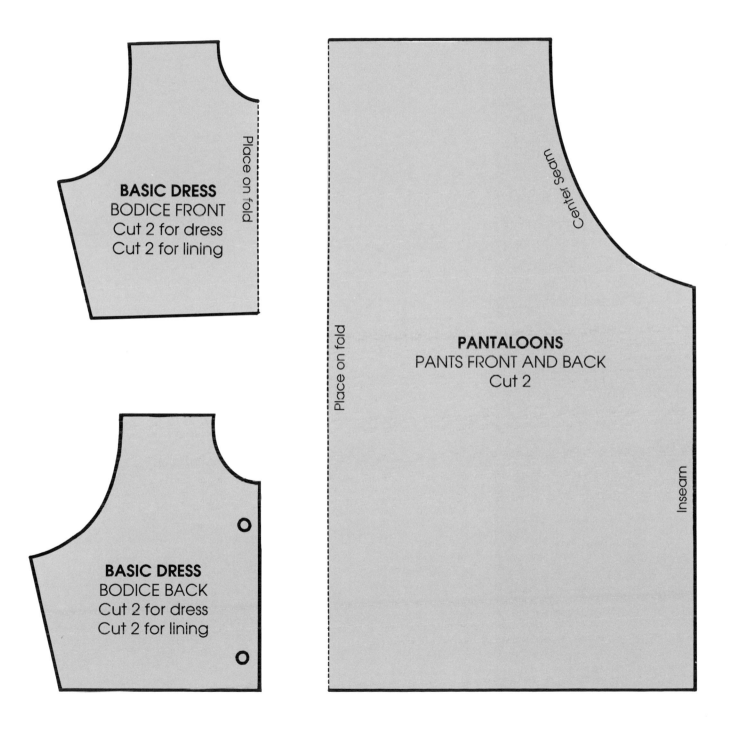

BASIC DRESS
BODICE FRONT
Cut 2 for dress
Cut 2 for lining

Place on fold

BASIC DRESS
BODICE BACK
Cut 2 for dress
Cut 2 for lining

PANTALOONS
PANTS FRONT AND BACK
Cut 2

Center Seam

Place on fold

Inseam

Shamrock Frock

Skirt: Stitched on mint green damask Aida 18 over one thread, the finished design size for one motif (double clover) is 1" x ⅜". The stitch count is 17 x 7. The fabric was cut 26" x 8". Stitch the design 3" from one 26" edge. Repeat motif 1" apart across entire 26" edge.

Jacket: Stitched on mint green damask Aida 18 over one thread, the finished design size for one half motif (single clover) is ⅜" x ⅜". The stitch count is 7 x 7. Trace jacket front pattern on fabric, then flip pattern and trace second jacket front piece. Center single clover designs so that they are ½" from edges of each rounded corner (see photo).

MATERIALS for dress and jacket:
¼ yard of mint green damask Aida 18 (includes completed cross-stitch designs for skirt and jacket); matching thread
Scraps of mint green fabric for lining
2½ yards of ⅛"-wide green ribbon
6"-8" of elastic thread
Two small snap sets
Green elf shoes (purchased at craft store)

DIRECTIONS:
All seam allowances are ¼". Instructions and patterns for BASIC DRESS are on pages 127-129.

1. For skirt, trim design piece to 24" x 6½" with lower edge of design 2" from 24" edge. Slipstitch one 24" piece of ribbon around skirt ¼" above design. Slipstitch two more parallel pieces of ribbon ¼" below design and ¼" apart.

2. Cut all BASIC DRESS pieces from unstitched Aida according to patterns. Complete Steps 2-8 of BASIC DRESS.

3. Cut JACKET FRONT, JACKET BACK and SLEEVE pieces from unstitched Aida according to patterns. Repeat with mint green fabric for lining.

4. With right sides of Aida jacket fronts and back together, stitch the shoulders. Repeat with lining pieces. Stitch jacket and jacket lining with right sides together, leaving side and sleeve seams open. Turn through one side seam.

5. Stitch two parallel 4" lengths of ribbon on one sleeve 1" from straight edge and ¼" apart. Turn end of sleeve under ½"; hem. Repeat for second sleeve. With right sides together, stitch sleeve cap to jacket. Stitch along one side seam and one sleeve. Repeat for second sleeve cap, side seam and sleeve.

Step One: Cross-stitch (one strand)

ANCHOR		DMC (used for sample)	
227		701	Christmas Green-lt.

Step Two: Backstitch (one strand)

246		895	Christmas Green-dk.

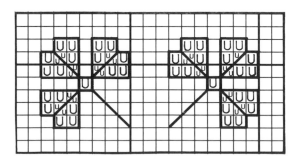

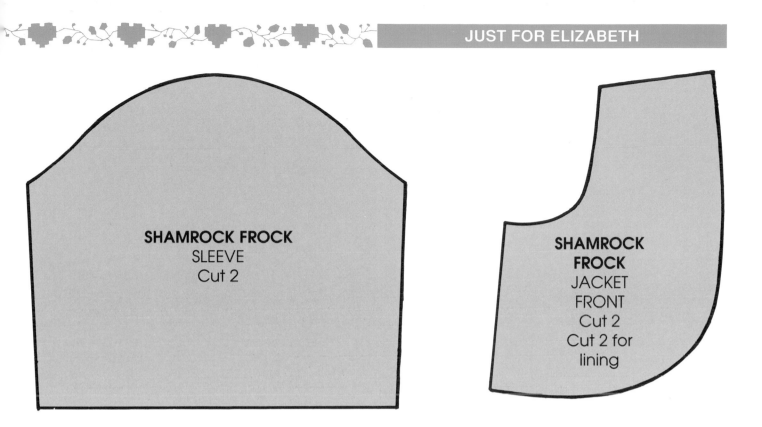

SHAMROCK FROCK
SLEEVE
Cut 2

**SHAMROCK
FROCK**
JACKET
FRONT
Cut 2
Cut 2 for
lining

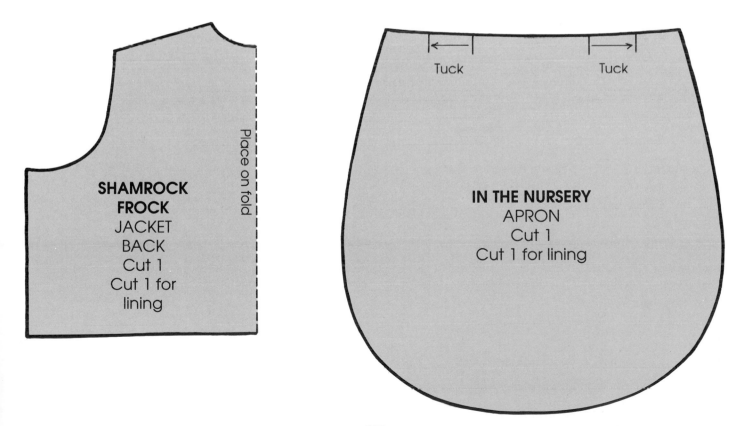

**SHAMROCK
FROCK**
JACKET
BACK
Cut 1
Cut 1 for
lining

Place on fold

Tuck

Tuck

IN THE NURSERY
APRON
Cut 1
Cut 1 for lining

Whispers of Spring

The design for the skirt is from "On the Back Porch" (pages 49-54). The flower motif contains the bottom left corner flowers, the flowers immediately to the right (centered between corner flowers), and the bottom right corner flowers (see photo). Stitched on ice blue damask Aida 18 over one thread, the finished design size is 7¼" x 2⅜". The stitch count is 130 x 43. The fabric was cut 12" x 9". Trace an 8" x 5" rectangle on unstitched Aida. Begin stitching center flowers ¾" above bottom 8" edge and centered horizontally. Elizabeth's apron is worn over a BASIC DRESS made from a cream floral print fabric (instructions and patterns on pages 127-129).

MATERIALS for apron:
¼ yard of ice blue damask Aida 18 (includes completed cross-stitch design on ice blue damask Aida 18; matching thread
Scraps of cream floral print fabric
One small snap set

DIRECTIONS:
All seam allowances are ¼".

1. Trim design piece to 8" x 5" (this will be the apron skirt). From unstitched Aida, cut one 1¾" x 2" piece for bib, two 7½" x 1" strips for waistband, and four ¾" x 5" strips for straps. From floral print fabric, cut one 8" x 5" piece for apron skirt lining, and one 1¾" x 1⅝" piece for bib lining. Cut RUFFLE pieces from unstitched Aida according to pattern. Repeat with print fabric for lining.

2. With right sides together, stitch apron skirt and lining together, leaving top edge open. Trim corners. Turn. Set aside.

3. To make bib, pintuck three ⅛"-deep horizontal rows, beginning ½" from 1¾" edge (top) of bib and spacing them ⅛" apart (see photo). With right sides together, stitch bib and lining across top edge. Turn and press. Set aside.

4. With right sides together, stitch ruffle and ruffle lining along curved edge. Clip curves. Turn. Stitch gathering threads on straight edge of ruffle/lining and gather to 4½". Repeat for other ruffle. Aligning raw edges, sandwich one ruffle between two strap strips with right sides together and with ruffle ¼" from both ends of strap (Diagram 1). Stitch long edge catching ruffle in seam. Trim seam allowances. Turn. Repeat for other strap.

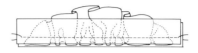

Diagram 1

5. Sandwich one edge of bib between strap strips, aligning all bottom edges. Fold raw edges of strap ¼" to the inside. Topstitch long edge and ends closed. Repeat with other side of bib and second strap.

6. Mark centers of lower edge of bib and both waistband strips on long edge. Sandwich bib between strips with right sides together, matching center marks. Stitch one long edge and ends of waistband. Clip corners. Turn waistband.

7. Stitch gathering threads in waist of apron skirt. Gather to 4". Mark center of waist edge of the skirt. Sandwich skirt between waistband strips with right sides together and matching centers. Fold raw edges of waistband under ¼". Slipstitch long edge. Tack ends of ruffles to back of waistband. Sew a snap set to ends of waistband.

WHISPERS OF SPRING
RUFFLE
Cut 2
Cut 2 for lining

Place on fold

In the Nursery

Skirt: Stitched on pink fabric using Waste Canvas 14 over one, the finished design size for one motif is 5⅝" x ¾". The stitch count is 79 x 11. The fabric was cut 26" x 8" and the waste canvas was cut 3" x 8". Stitch the design so that the bottom edge of the motif is 2" from one 26" edge. Repeat the motif across entire 26" edge.

Sleeves: Stitched on pink fabric using Waste Canvas 14 over one thread, the finished design size for one half motif (triangle) is 5⅝" x ⅜". The fabric was cut 7" x 6" and the waste canvas was cut 7" x 2". The stitch count is 79 x 6. Trace two sleeve patterns before stitching. Stitch design so that straight edge of triangle border is 2" from wrist edge (top point of triangle points toward wrist edge).

MATERIALS for dress, apron and headband:
¼ yard of pink fabric (includes completed cross-stitch designs for skirt and sleeves); matching thread
Scraps of white fabric for apron; matching thread
30" of 1"-wide gathered lace trim
One 1" piece of ⅛"-wide elastic
6"-8" of elastic thread

DIRECTIONS:
All seam allowances are ¼". Instructions and patterns for BASIC dress are on pages 127-129.

1. For skirt, trim design piece to 24" x 6½" with bottom edge of design 1½" from 24" edge. For sleeves, cut design pieces according to BASIC DRESS sleeve pattern with straight edge of design 1¾" from wrist edge. Cut remaining BASIC DRESS pieces from pink fabric according to patterns.

2. Complete Steps 2-8 of BASIC DRESS.

3. Cut APRON pieces from white fabric according to pattern(page 131). Also from white fabric cut one 3½" x 2" piece for bib and one 24" x 1" piece for sash. From lace, cut one 12" piece for apron, two 6" pieces for shoulder straps and one 5" piece for headband.

4. With right sides together and matching straight edges, stitch one 12" piece of lace around apron front

Step One: Cross-stitch (one strand)

ANCHOR		DMC (used for sample)	
300	–	745	Yellow-lt. pale
4146	o	754	Peach-lt.
48	·	818	Baby Pink
50	X	605	Cranberry-vy. lt.
108	▢	211	Lavender-lt.
128	●	800	Delft-pale
206	∴	955	Nile Green-lt.

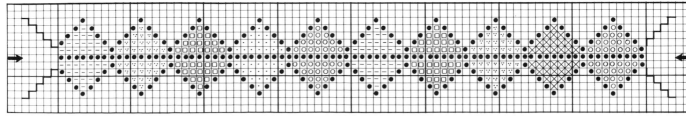

from top left corner, around curved edges to top right. With right sides together and lace sandwiched between, stitch apron front and back pieces together, leaving top edge open. Turn. Set aside.

5. For bib, fold 3½" x 2" piece in half to equal 1¾" x 2". Stitch along both 1¾" edges. Trim seam allowances. Turn. Stitch one 6" piece of lace to bib front at each 1¾" edge, leaving 4¼" tails at the top of bib. Set aside.

6. Fold two tucks in waist edge of apron; see pattern. With right sides together, stitch bib to apron sewing

across lace on both sides. Fold the 24" x 1" piece in half to equal ½" wide. Stitch along long edge. Turn. Slipstitch ends closed. Press so that seam is in center back. Mark center of bib/apron and sash. Place sash over front of apron at bib/apron seam, matching center marks. Stitch along lower edge of sash across apron front and lace. Place apron on doll and adjust lace shoulder straps, marking placement on back of sash. Tack ends of straps to sash. Tack elastic to each end of 5" piece of lace for headband. Place on doll head (see photo).

Country Smock

The design for the heart pocket is from "All Around Town" (pages 63-68). The house/heart motif is the third heart from the left on the sampler. Stitched on Quaker Cloth 28 over two threads, the finished design size is 2½" x 2¼". The stitch count is 35 x 32. The fabric was cut 6" x 6". Elizabeth's smock is worn over a peach and white print BASIC DRESS (instructions and patterns are on pages 127-129).

MATERIALS for smock:
¼ yard of Quaker Cloth 28 (includes completed cross-stitch design); matching thread
¼ yard of peach and white print fabric for lining
One small snap set

DIRECTIONS:
All seam allowances are ¼".

1. Trim design piece ¼" outside stitching. Cut SMOCK pieces from unstitched Quaker Cloth according to pattern (page 136). Also from unstitched Quaker Cloth, cut 1"-wide bias, piecing as needed, to equal 6". Cut lining pieces from print fabric according to SMOCK pattern. Also from print fabric, cut one heart for lining, using design piece for pattern and one 4½" square piece for handkerchief.

2. With right sides of smock front and two back pieces together, stitch shoulder seams. Then stitch the side seams. Repeat with lining pieces.

3. With right sides together, stitch design piece to heart lining piece, leaving an opening. Turn. Slipstitch opening closed. Place heart on left side of smock 2" from the bottom and 1" from the side seam. Whipstitch around heart, leaving the top open to make a pocket.

4. Place right sides of smock and lining together, matching the side and shoulder seams. Stitch the center back edges and bottom edge. Turn.

5. Fold the raw edges of the armholes to the inside, clipping as needed; slipstitch.

(continued on next page)

6. Treating smock and lining as one piece, stitch gathering threads around neck. Gather neckline to fit bias, placing all fullness near the center front. With right sides together, stitch bias to smock front around neckline. Fold ¼" double to inside of smock; slipstitch. Fold raw edges of bias ends to inside and slipstitch closed.

7. Sew the snap set to the neck at the center back. For handkerchief, fray ends of 4½" square of fabric. Place in heart pocket (see photo).

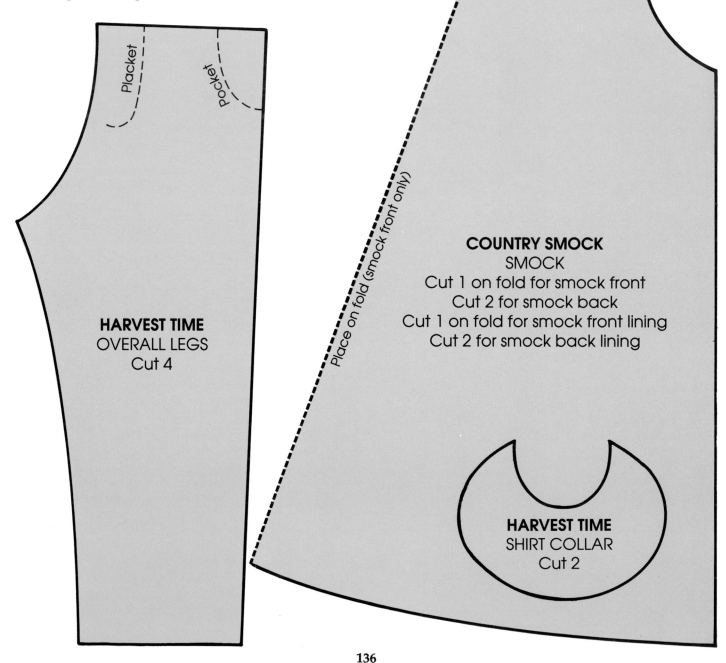

Placket

pocket

HARVEST TIME
OVERALL LEGS
Cut 4

Place on fold (smock front only)

COUNTRY SMOCK
SMOCK
Cut 1 on fold for smock front
Cut 2 for smock back
Cut 1 on fold for smock front lining
Cut 2 for smock back lining

HARVEST TIME
SHIRT COLLAR
Cut 2

Harvest Time

The design for the bib is from "Homegrown Happiness" (pages 92-97). The motif is the middle piece of corn in the top right corner of the sampler. Stitched on white Hardanger 22 over one thread, the finished design size is ⅞" x 1½". The stitch count is 18 x 32. The fabric was cut 5" x 6".

MATERIALS for shirt and overalls:
Completed cross-stitch design on white Hardanger 22
⅛ yard of red/white ¹⁄₁₆" gingham; matching thread
¼ yard of lightweight denim; matching thread
6"-8" of elastic thread
Orange thread for topstitching
Two ⅛" gold beads
Four small snap sets

DIRECTIONS for shirt:
All seam allowances are ¼". Instructions and patterns for BASIC DRESS are on pages 127-129.

1. To make the shirt, cut the bodice front and backs from gingham according to BASIC DRESS patterns, adding 1" to waist edges. Cut sleeves from gingham according to BASIC DRESS pattern. Cut SHIRT COLLAR pieces from gingham according to pattern (left).

2. Stitch right sides of two collar pieces together along curved edge. Turn. Repeat with remaining pieces.

3. With right sides of one bodice front and two bodice back pieces together, stitch the shoulders. Repeat for lining. Match collar pieces at center front and baste to the right side of bodice front.

4. Complete Steps 3-5 of BASIC DRESS.

5. Fold bottom edge of shirt under ¼" double to wrong side and hem. Sew three snap sets to center back opening, spacing them evenly.

DIRECTIONS for overalls:
All seam allowances are ¼".

1. To make the bib, trim the design piece to 1½" x 2⅛", centering design. From denim, cut one 1½" x 1" and two 1" x 2¾" pieces.

2. Stitch 1½" piece to top of design piece with right sides together. Press seam open. Topstitch on denim close to design piece with orange thread. With right sides together, stitch one 2¾" piece to each side of design piece, overlapping denim strip and aligning at top. Press seams open. Topstitch these strips close to design piece.

3. From denim, cut one piece the same size as the bib front and two 5½" x 1" strips for waistband.

4. With right sides together, stitch bib front and back, leaving bottom edge open. Clip corners. Turn. Topstitch close to outside edges of denim (see photo).

5. Mark centers of lower edge of bib and both waistband strips on long edge. Sandwich bib between strips with right sides together, matching center marks. Stitch one long edge and ends of waistband. Clip corners. Turn waistband. Set aside.

6. To make pants, cut OVERALL LEGS from denim according to pattern. Topstitch the pockets on the right and left pants front, and the placket on the left pants front (see pattern). With right sides of one front and back leg piece together, stitch the side seam. Topstitch along side seam. Repeat with remaining leg pieces.

(continued on next page)

7. Fold ankle edges of legs under ¼" double to wrong side; stitch. Topstitch ankle hems.

8. With right sides together, stitch inseams. Press seams open. Put one leg inside the other with right sides together (Diagram 1). Stitch center seam, stitching the center back seam to within 1½" of the top edge. Press seam open. Turn.

9. With right sides together, stitch legs to waistband, matching one edge of waistband with opening in pants, leaving ½" extension for snap on opposite edge. Turn. Topstitch all edges of waistband.

Diagram 1

10. To make straps, cut two 1¼" x 4½" pieces for straps. Fold pieces to measure ⅝" wide. Stitch long edge. Turn. Topstitch close to each edge. Tack strap ends to back side of bib. Sew gold beads to front of bib (see photo). Place overalls on doll. Cross straps in back. Tack ends inside waistband. Sew a snap set to ends of waistband, adjusting to fit doll.

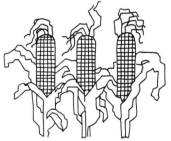

THE SLEIGH RIDE
CAPE
Cut 1 from design piece
Cut 1 from unstitched sky blue fabric

Place on fold

See code on page 139

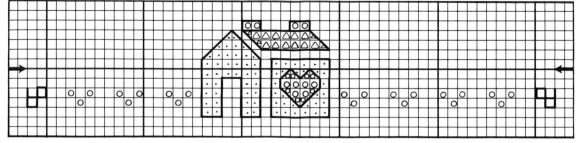

138

The Cat's Meow

Skirt: Stitched on Waste Canvas 20 over one, the finished design size for one house/heart motif is 3¼" x ¾". The stitch count is 46 x 10. The fabric was cut 26" x 8". Repeat motif (page 138) across entire 26" edge. (See Step 1 of directions for placement.)

Bodice: Stitched on Waste Canvas 20 over one, the finished design size for the heart border is ¼" x 2⅝". The stitch count is 3 x 37. Before stitching, trace bodice pattern onto fabric. Design (left) is centered 1" below neckline.

Step One: Cross-stitch (one strand)

ANCHOR		DMC (used for sample)
11		3328 Salmon-dk.
922		930 Antique Blue-dk.
942		738 Tan-vy. lt.

Step Two: Backstitch (one strand)

339		920 Copper-med.

MATERIALS for dress:
¼ yard of white fabric (includes completed cross-stitch designs for bodice and skirt); matching thread
Scraps of white permanent pleat nylon
1 yard of ½"-wide lace trim
Four small snap sets

DIRECTIONS:
All seam allowances are ¼". Instructions and patterns for BASIC DRESS are on pages 127-129.

1. Trim design piece for skirt to 24" x 4½" with design 1" from 24" edge. Cut BODICE FRONT and BACKS from white fabric according to BASIC DRESS, adding 1" to waist edges. Cut SLEEVES from white fabric according to BASIC DRESS, subtracting 1" from wrist edges. Complete Steps 2-3 of BASIC DRESS.

2. For sleeves, cut one 2½" x 1½" piece of permanent pleat nylon. Cut one 5½" and one 2" piece of lace. Sew one piece of lace to each 2 ½" edge of pleated nylon with a zigzag stitch, stretching or gathering pleats to fit lace. (The 2" piece of lace will be the cuff.) Place 5½" edge of lace/pleated nylon ⅛" over straight edge of one sleeve piece. Sew with a zigzag stitch. Repeat for second sleeve (see photo).

3. Stitch gathering threads in sleeve cap. Gather sleeve to fit armhole. Stitch the sleeve cap to the bodice. Repeat with second sleeve. With right sides together, stitch one side seam and one sleeve. Repeat for the remaining side seam and sleeve.

4. To make collar, cut one 6½" x 1½" piece of pleated nylon. Cut one 14" piece and one 3½" piece from lace. Sew one piece of lace to each 6½" edge of pleated nylon with zigzag stitch. Sew collar to bodice at neckline with zigzag stitch so that the 3½" piece of lace is ¼" above neckline (see photo). Complete Steps 6-8 of BASIC DRESS. Sew snaps on the center back opening, spacing them evenly.

DIRECTIONS for upright cats:
Both cat designs are taken from "One Summer Afternoon" (pages 80-86) and are stitched on white Belfast Linen 32 over two threads. After stitching, stiffen them with fabric stiffener.

Black/white cat: The finished design size is 2¼" x 1". The stitch count is 35 x 17.

Orange cat: The finished design size is 1¼" x 2". The stitch count is 19 x 31.

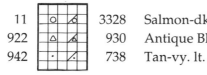

The Sleigh Ride

Skirt: The design for the skirt is from "Christmas Homecoming" (pages 111-116). The horse and sleigh motif is in the middle right section of the sampler. Stitched on sky blue fabric using Waste Canvas 14 over one, the finished design size is 3⅞" x 1⅞". The stitch count is 54 x 26. The fabric was cut 24" x 8½". The waste canvas was cut 6" x 4". Stitch the motif so that the bottom edge is 2½" from the bottom edge of the fabric and centered horizontally.

Cape: Stitched on sky blue fabric using Waste Canvas 14 over one, the finished design size for one motif is 1⅜" x 1⅛". The fabric and waste canvas were cut 9" x 6½". Trace cape pattern on waste canvas, then repeat motif to fill pattern using DMC white floss.

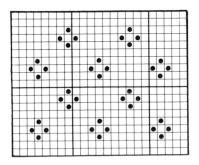

MATERIALS for dress, cape, hat and muff:
⅜ yard of sky blue fabric (includes completed cross-stitch designs for skirt and cape); matching thread
Scraps of white fake fur
1 yard of ⅛"-wide sky blue satin ribbon
Two small snap sets
6"-8" of elastic thread
Glue

DIRECTIONS:
All seam allowances are ¼". Instructions and patterns for BASIC DRESS are on pages 127-129.

1. To make dress, trim design piece for skirt 24" x 6½", with design ½" above bottom 24" edge and centered horizontally. Cut all BASIC DRESS pieces from blue fabric according to patterns. Complete Steps 2-8 of BASIC DRESS.

2. To make cape, cut CAPE pieces according to pattern(page 138). From fur cut one 30" x 1" piece. Fold fur strip in half, with fur side out, to measure ½". Stitch fur to right side of cape design piece with raw edges aligned. With right sides of design piece and lining together, stitch all edges, leaving an opening. Clip corners. Turn. Slipstitch opening closed.

3. Cut two 10" pieces of ribbon. Fold one piece into three ½"-deep loops, leaving a 7" tail. Tack to upper right at neck in a clover-like arrangement. Repeat with second piece of ribbon, tacking to upper left at neck. Place cape on doll and tie tails of ribbon in a bow to secure. Tack lower edges of cape together under each arm.

4. To make hat, cut one 4¾"-wide circle and one 2" x 7" strip for hatband from blue fabric. Also cut one 6" x ½" strip of fur. Fold fabric strip in half to equal 3½" wide. Stitch along 2" ends. Turn. Fold in half to equal 1" x 3"; press. (This will be the hatband.) Stitch gathering threads around circle. Gather circle to fit hatband. With right sides together and matching raw edges, stitch circle to hatband. Glue strip of fur around outside of hatband. Cut small, circular piece of fur for pompom and glue to center top of hat.

5. To make muff, cut one 2½" x 4½" piece from fur. Cut one 2½" x 4½" piece from blue fabric for lining. Stitch fur to fabric with right sides together, leaving an opening. Turn. Slipstitch opening closed. Fold in half with right sides together to equal 2". Slipstitch along 2" edge opposite fold. Turn. Cut one 12" piece of ribbon. Slide ribbon through muff and tie ends in knot.

Cross-Stitch

Fabrics: Counted cross-stitch is usually worked on even-weave fabric. These fabrics are manufactured specifically for counted thread embroidery and are woven with the same number of vertical as horizontal threads per inch. Because the number of threads in the fabric is equal in each direction, each stitch will be the same size. It is the number of threads per inch in even-weave fabrics that determines the size of a finished design.

Waste Canvas: Cut the waste canvas 1" larger on all sides than the finished design size. Baste the waste canvas to the fabric to be stitched. Complete the stitching. Then, dampen the stitched area with cold water. Pull the waste canvas threads out one at a time with tweezers. It is easier to pull all the threads running in one direction first, then pull out the opposite threads. Allow the stitching to dry. Place face down on a towel and iron.

Preparing fabric: Cut even-weave fabric at least 3" larger on all sides than the design size, or cut it the size specified in the sample paragraph. A 3" margin is the minimum amount of space that allows for working the edges of the design comfortably. If the item is to be finished into a sachet bag, for example, the fabric should be cut as directed. To keep fabric from fraying, whipstitch or machine zigzag the raw edges.

Needles: Needles should slip easily through the holes in the fabric, but not pierce the fabric. Use a blunt tapestry needle, size 24 or 26. Never leave the needle in the design area of your work. It can leave rust or a permanent impression on your fabric.

Floss: All numbers and color names are cross referenced between ANCHOR and DMC brands of floss. Run the floss over a damp sponge to straighten. Separate all six strands and use the number of strands called for in the code.

Centering design: Find the center of the fabric by folding it in half horizontally and then vertically. Place a pin in the fold point to mark the center. Locate the center of the design on the graph by following the vertical and horizontal arrows. Begin stitching at the center point of the graph and the fabric.

Graphs: When a graph is continued, the bottom two rows of the graph on the previous page are repeated, separated by a small space, indicating where to connect them.

Securing the floss: Start by inserting your needle up from the underside of the fabric at your starting point. Hold 1" of thread behind the fabric and stitch over it, securing with the first few stitches. To finish thread, run under four or more stitches on the back of the design. Never knot floss unless working on clothing.

Another method for securing floss is the waste knot. Knot your floss and insert your needle from the right side of the fabric about 1" from the design area. Work several stitches over the thread to secure. Cut off the knot later.

Stitching: For a smooth cross-stitch, use the "push and pull" method. Push the needle straight down and completely through fabric before pulling. Do not pull the thread tight. The tension should be consistent throughout, making the stitches even. Make one stitch for every symbol on the chart. To stitch in rows, work from left to right and then back. Half-crosses are used to make a rounded shape. Make the longer stitch in the direction of the slanted line.

Carrying floss: To carry floss, weave floss under the previously worked stitches on the back. Do not carry your thread across any fabric that is not or will not be stitched. Loose threads, especially dark ones, will show through the fabric.

Twisted floss: If floss is twisted, drop the needle and allow the floss to unwind itself. Floss will cover best when lying flat. Use thread no longer than 18" because it will tend to twist and knot.

Cleaning completed work: When all stitching is complete, soak the completed work in cold water with a mild soap for 5 to 10 minutes. Rinse and roll work into a towel to remove excess water; do not wring. Place work face down on a dry towel and, with iron on a warm setting, iron until work is dry.

Stitches

Cross-stitch: Make one cross for each symbol on the chart. Bring needle and thread up at A, down at B, up at C, and down again at D.

For rows, stitch from left to right, then back. All stitches should lie in the same direction.

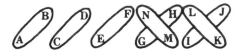

Half-cross: Make the longer stitch in the direction of the slanted line on the graph. The stitch actually fits three-fourths of the area. Bring needle and thread up at A, down at B, up at C, and down at D.

Backstitch: Complete all cross-stitching before working back stitches or other accent stitches. Working from left to right with one strand of floss (unless designated otherwise in code), bring needle and thread up at A, down at B, and up again at C. Going back down at A, continue in this manner.

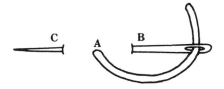

French Knot: Bring the needle up at A, using one strand of embroidery floss. Wrap floss around needle two times (unless indicated otherwise in instructions). Insert needle beside A, pulling floss until it fits snugly around needle. Pull needle through to back.

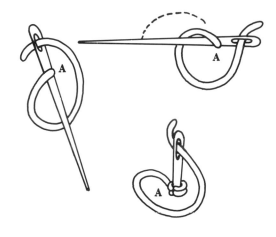

Beadwork: Attach beads to fabric with a half-cross, lower left to upper right. Secure beads by returning thread through beads, lower right to upper left. Complete row of half-crosses before returning to secure all beads.

Sewing Hints

Patterns: Use tracing paper to trace the patterns. Be sure to transfer all information. All patterns include seam allowances. The seam allowance is ¼" unless otherwise specified.

Marking on fabric: Always use a dressmakers' pen or chalk to mark on fabric. It will wash out when you clean your finished piece.

Gathering: Machine-stitch two parallel rows of long stitches ¼" and ½" from the edge of the fabric (unless instructions say differently). Leave the ends of the thread 2" or 3" long. Pull the two bobbin threads and gather to fit the desired length. Long edges may need to be gathered from both ends. Disperse the fullness evenly and secure the threads in the area by wrapping them around a pin in a figure eight.

Slipstitch: Insert needle at A, slide it through the folded edge of the fabric for about ⅛" to ¼" and bring it out at B. Directly below B, take a small stitch through the second piece of fabric.

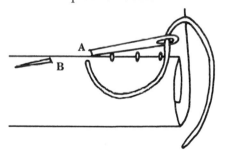

Enlarging a pattern: On a 15" x 20" sheet of paper, mark grid lines 1" apart to fill the paper. Begin marking dots on 1" grid lines where the reduced pattern intersects the corresponding grid line. Connect the dots.

Bias strips: Bias strips are used for ruffles, binding, or corded piping. To cut bias, fold the fabric at a 45-degree angle to the grain of the fabric and crease. Cut on the crease. Cut additional strips the width indicated in the instructions and parallel to the first cutting line. The ends of the bias strips should be on the grain of the fabric. Place the right sides of the ends together and stitch with a ¼" seam. Continue to piece the strips until they are the length that is indicated in the instructions.

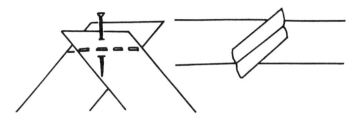

Suppliers

All products are available retail from Shepherd's Bush, 220 24th Street, Ogden, UT 84401; 801-399-4546. Or, for a merchant near you, write to the following suppliers:

Zweigart Fabrics:
Aida 18 (black, white), **Belfast Linen 32** (cream, driftwood, ivory, raw linen, white), **Damask Aida 14** (ice blue, ivory, mint green), **Dublin Linen 25** (dirty linen, raw linen, yellow), **Murano 30** (white), **Quaker Cloth 28**

Zweigart/Joan Toggit Ltd.
35 Fairfield Place
West Caldwell, NJ 07006

Elizabeth Porcelain Doll Parts, Easter Screen
Chapelle Designers, Box 9252 Newgate Station, Ogden, UT 84409, (801) 621-2777

Crepe Hair
All Cooped Up Patterns
212 So. State St., #204
Orem, UT 84058, (801) 226-1517

Mill Hill Beads
Gay Bowles Sales, Inc.
1310 Plainfield Avenue
P.O. Box 1060
Janesville, WI 53547, (800) 356-9438

Balger Blending Filament
Kreinik Manufacturing
P.O. Box 1966
Parkersburg, WV 26101

INDEX

All of us at Meredith® Press are dedicated to offering you, our customer, the best books we can create. We are particularly concerned that all of the instructions for making projects are clear and accurate. Please address your correspondence to Customer Service Department, Meredith® Press, Meredith Corporation, 150 East 52nd Street, New York, NY 10022.

Home Is Where the Heart Is: An American Sampler 1991 is the third in a series of cross-stitch books. If you would like the first two books in the series, *Quilt Designs in Cross-Stitch: An American Sampler 1989*, and *Country Cross-Stitch Designs: An American Sampler 1990*, please write to Better Homes and Gardens Books, P.O. Box 10670, Des Moines, Iowa 50336, or call 1-800-678-2665.

For information on how you can have *Better Homes and Gardens* delivered to your door, write to: Mr. Robert Austin, P.O. Box 4536, Des Moines, IA 50336.